Critical Guides to French

DATE DUE FOR RETURN

116 Bernanos: Journal d'un curé de campagne

Critical Guides to French Texts

EDITED BY ROGER LITTLE, WOLFGANG VAN EMDEN, DAVID WILLIAMS

BERNANOS

Journal d'un curé de campagne

Malcolm Scott

Professor of French
University of St Andrews

Grant & Cutler Ltd
1997

DEPÓSITO LEGAL: V. 354 - 1997

Printed in Spain by
Artes Gráficas Soler, S.A., Valencia
for
GRANT & CUTLER LTD
55-57 GREAT MARLBOROUGH STREET, LONDON W1V 2AY

Contents

Prefatory Note

For reasons stated in the first chapter of this guide, references to *Journal d'un curé de campagne* are followed by a double set of page numbers. The first number relates to the preferred critical edition: *Œuvres romanesques*, Bibliothèque de la Pléiade (Gallimard, 1980), edited by Albert Béguin, with notes by Michel Estève and preface by Gaëtan Picon; the second to the Pocket edition (1994), which is the most easily available current paperback edition.

References to other novels and sundry writings by Bernanos, unless otherwise indicated, are to the Pléiade edition, and are followed by one single page number.

References to other books are shown by italicised numbers in parentheses which refer to works in the Select Bibliography.

I am grateful to Monsieur Jean-Loup Bernanos for permission to consult the manuscript of the novel in the Bibliothèque Nationale, Paris, and to him and his wife, Mme Brigitte Bernanos, for their encouragement of my work and for information on the topography of Bernanos's 'Ambricourt imaginaire'.

Introduction

Journal d'un curé de campagne was published by Editions Plon on March 17th 1936, heralded by an eleven-part abridged version in *La Revue hebdomadaire* between the previous December and February (*9* (a), p.9). The novel had an instant success, confirmed by its winning the Grand Prix du Roman de l'Académie Française. As letters to his friend Robert Vallery-Radot testify, Bernanos began writing the novel in the last few weeks of 1934 (*8*, II, pp.44, 124), but its composition was not continuous. After drafting the first fifty pages, Bernanos was soon forced to suspend the project in favour of *Un crime*, a would-be detective story which he published in 1935 in the hope of stabilising his financial situation. These same financial pressures had already caused him to move with his wife and family to Majorca, where living was cheaper. It was there, in Palma, and more specifically, in keeping with his ingrained habit and preference, in two cafés, the Borne and the Alhambra (*10* (a), p.7), that his best-known novel was written, principally in two bursts of activity at either end of the fourteen-month period from late 1934, and interspersed with work on two further novels, *Un mauvais rêve* (published posthumously in 1950) and *Monsieur Ouine*, which he completed and published during another period of voluntary exile, in Brazil, in 1943. The years in Majorca, artistically fruitful, were in other respects traumatic, for Bernanos witnessed there the early phase of the Spanish Civil War, an experience which inspired *Les Grands Cimetières sous la lune* (1938), one of the works of political polemic on which, as well as on his eight novels, his reputation as a writer is founded. Finally, it was also in Majorca that he conceived the idea of writing yet another novel, *Nouvelle histoire de Mouchette* (1937).

Georges Bernanos had emerged as a novelist at a relatively mature age, not far short of his fortieth year, producing in quick succession *Sous le soleil de Satan* (1926), *L'Imposture* (1927) and *La Joie* (1929), the last winning the Prix Fémina. There followed his first major polemical work, *La Grande Peur des bien-pensants* (1931). Before becoming a full-time writer, he had returned from service in the First World War to work as an insurance salesman, while maintaining the involvement in right-wing politics which had developed in his pre-war student days, and which had brought him into the circle of Charles Maurras and Léon Daudet, the intellectual leaders of the monarchist movement L'Action Française. Despite a painful break with Maurras in 1932, he continued to share the latter's critical view of the liberalising spirit of modern France, which he saw as both source and symptom of national decadence, and indeed of the whole trend of French history since the Revolution. He was particularly opposed, as a Catholic, to the progressive movements within the Church which he regarded as collaboration, under a tepidly conservative guise, in a process of secularisation; and he campaigned instead for a counter-revolutionary restoration of traditional values. His open letter, 'Adieu, Maurras!', was forced upon him by the personal agnosticism of the leader of a movement which drew much of its support from Catholics, a situation which had led to the denunciation of the Action Française by the Vatican in 1926, and which became increasingly intolerable for the deeply religious Bernanos.

Catholic faith was indeed the bedrock of all that Bernanos wrote or did. Born in Paris in 1888 into an intensely devout middle-class family, the young Bernanos studied at the seminary of Aire-sur-la-Lys as the first step to his intended ordination. Although this early vocation was abandoned, the priest's mission exerted a life-long fascination for him. His first three novels have priests as their central characters and the theological conflicts of good and evil as their themes. *Journal d'un curé de campagne*, he announced to Vallery-Radot, would also be the story of a priest and the struggles of his ministry, and it would exemplify the central Christian message of salvation in the face of failure and death:

J'ai commencé un beau vieux livre, que vous aimerez, je

crois. J'ai résolu de faire le journal d'un jeune prêtre, à son entrée dans une paroisse. Il va chercher midi à quatorze heures, se démener comme quatre, faire des projets mirifiques, qui échoueront naturellement, se laisser plus ou moins duper par des imbéciles, des vicieuses ou des salauds et alors qu'il croira tout perdu, il aura servi le bon Dieu dans la mesure même ou il croira l'avoir desservi. Sa naïveté aura eu raison de tout, et il mourra tranquillement d'un cancer.

(*8*, II, pp.46-47)

Yet, more than any other of his novels, it came to occupy a unique place in his heart. 'J'aime ce livre comme s'il n'était pas de moi,' he wrote (p.1879). 'J'y tiens énormément,' he echoed in a letter to his editor. 'Je crois être sûr de lui. Je le crois appelé à retentir dans beaucoup d'êtres, et je n'ai d'ailleurs jamais fait, même de loin, un tel effort de dépouillement, de sincérité, de sérénité pour les atteindre' (p.1878). This special attachment to his novel arose from a number of sources, including its evocation of the landscapes of his childhood, of '[les] chemins du pays d'Artois', the region in the extreme north of France which he recalls so fondly in the preface to *Les Grands Cimetières sous la lune* (*7*, p.355). The real place names mentioned in the *Journal* – Montreuil, Fruges, Hesdin, Heuchin, Desvres, Norenfontes, Verchocq, Torcy – identify the area as the south-western fringe of the department of Pas-de-Calais. There is even a hamlet called Ambricourt, situated a few kilometres to the east of the old battle site of Azincourt (or Agincourt), but the Ambricourt of the novel is based on transposed memories of the village of Fressin, where his family had their country house and where Bernanos spent his boyhood holidays. He confirmed to a correspondent that the *châtelain* of Fressin had suggested to him certain aspects of two of his characters: the count and, less obviously, the curé de Torcy (p.1879). But more important still was his closeness to the character of the curé of Ambricourt himself, whom he addresses as follows in the preface mentioned above: 'Vous, vous seul de mes créatures dont j'ai cru parfois distinguer le visage, mais à qui je n'ai pas osé donner de nom – cher curé d'un Ambricourt imaginaire' (7, p.355).

Bernanos's earlier fictional priests had been of a wide variety. The first, in *Sous le soleil de Satan*, was the abbé Donissan, known as 'le saint de Lumbres' because of a life-time of heroic struggle against the devil. Next, in both *L'Imposture* and *La Joie*, appeared the intellectual priest Cénabre, a satirical though tragic representation of the Church's complicity with progressive historical and philosophical ideas, and his saintly opposite, the simple abbé Chevance. The curé d'Ambricourt can be compared or contrasted with these three predecessors. He shares with Donissan his humble social origins, awkwardness and sense of inadequacy, all of which cloak a profound spiritual vocation, and with Chevance his childlike meekness; and, like Cénabre, he is both a priest and, in his own way, a writer, although diametrically opposed to him in terms of the aims and product of the writing process. Another important priestly character is the curé de Fenouille, in *Monsieur Ouine*, begun before the *Journal* but finished later, in whom critics have seen a first sketch of the curé d'Ambricourt. None of these portraits, however, satisfied Bernanos as much as the hero of the *Journal*.

However, a reader of today might wonder whether there is much to engage the interest in a novel about a priest, especially a priest immersed in social and spiritual matters in the apparently remote context of 1930s France. More broadly, Bernanos's Christian and specifically Catholic preoccupations might be seen as a deterrent by readers born into what he saw as an increasingly dechristianised world. Concepts central to his vision of life, such as the theological virtues of faith, hope and charity, or doctrines which are reflected in the novel itself, like that of the Communion of Saints, have less currency than they once did, and a decreasing level of familiarity with the New Testament might render the contemporary reader less sensitive to the novel's biblical allusions and references. Yet Bernanos was very much a man of this world. His decision not to enter the priesthood was taken on the grounds that 'un laïque peut lutter sur bien des terrains où l'ecclésiastique ne peut pas faire grand-chose' (letter to abbé Lagrange, p.1730). This included the world of politics, where his passionate denunciation of injustice raises issues as relevant in our day as in his. He was never a spokesman for his Church, and none of his books was published by a Catholic publisher, though there were many such in France before the last war. There is no cloying sentimentality or facile piety about his writing, which is marked on the contrary by a vigorous refusal of easy answers based on mere emotional reactions. As a writer, his strategy was always to begin from the most concrete of human situations and to reveal the spiritual truths which he was convinced lay beneath them. He coined the phrase 'le réalisme catholique' (*6/7*, p.1039) to describe what he hoped to achieve by this strategy. The realism of classic French novelists like Balzac (whose *Comédie humaine* he otherwise deeply admired) lacked, he argued, a dimension which was nevertheless the most vital part of the 'real': the invisible, supernatural dimension of human life which is only accessible to us by communion with God through Christ – and even then not necessarily completely or in ways which our limited human minds can understand or our language express.

This guide will follow a strategy parallel to that of Bernanos: to work from what is most apparent in his description of the experiences and thoughts of his fictional characters towards an interpretation of the spiritual and – he would have said – 'supernatural' dramas that lie beneath this surface. It will begin with a consideration of the *Journal*'s essential formal difference from all his other novels: namely, the fact that it is written in the shape of a diary. The diary form already begins to alleviate the problem mentioned above, that of the reader for whom the special nature of priestly experience might at first glance present a daunting obstacle to empathy. From the first paragraph of the novel, we see the world of the young curé from within. Through his eyes and his words we experience his situation and encounter the social and religious problems, not just of this particular priest and his parish, but of the wider world on to which his first-person meditations open. And through the promptings of the novelist we become aware also of the spiritual meaning of a mission which the priest himself perhaps never fully understands.

1. A Novel and a Diary

(i) Reconstructing the text

We know that we are about to read a novel, yet the title tells us that it is also a diary. Such conflicting signals as to the nature of the text before us can disconcert. Will it have the fragmented, unstructured and improvised style of a typical diary, recording events, big and small, as they happen in series of brief, erratic and semi-obscure jottings, as diaries usually do? Or will it have the qualities that we would expect of a novel: a premeditated narrative, insights into a range of characters, a strong thematic structure, with perhaps a broader philosophical or social resonance, and a feel of aesthetic completeness? What should we expect of this text, and what reading strategy do we have to adopt to derive the greatest possible pleasure and satisfaction from reading it?

This *Journal* is clearly a novel. As we read it, we may gradually extrapolate from it a coherent plot which we can summarise as follows. It is the story of a country priest aged about thirty, who has just arrived to take up a new ministry in the parish of Ambricourt. It relates, by brief allusion rather than by full description, the routine aspects of his ministry: masses, confessions, funerals, catechism classes, and his attempts to organise a young people's club. In greater detail, it records his encounters with a number of particular individuals: with other members of the clergy, especially the priest from the neighbouring parish of Torcy, through whom he makes the acquaintance of the semi-retired doctor Delbende; with numerous members of the community with whom his work and daily life bring him into regular contact: his housekeeper Mme Pégriot, local merchants like the Pamyres, the sacristan M. Dumouchel and his young daughter Séraphita, the gravedigger

Arsène Miron, the gardener Clovis, his pupil Sylvestre Galuchet, a young house-painter called Sulpice Mitonnet; and, with increasing frequency, with the household of the local aristocrats, the unnamed count and countess, their daughter Chantal, the governess Mlle Louise, and the countess's nephew, Olivier. As he immerses himself in the lives of these parishioners, and especially in the tragedy of the loveless family of the count and countess, the curé's personal difficulties are also revealed. The reader learns of his sense of personal failure in his attempts to represent the Church within the community, of the pain he feels at the hostility of the villagers towards him, of the spiritual crisis in which even prayer becomes difficult, and of his deteriorating physical health. These factors, which are the essential materials of the book, gather momentum from its approximate half-way stage: Delbende dies, apparently by his own hand, the story of the countess reaches its climax in a scene which precedes her death and is also of profound personal significance to the curé, the latter goes to Lille to consult a doctor, a last journey which introduces other important characters – the doctor himself, Laville, and the curé's former seminarian friend Dufréty, in whose arms the curé dies.

This story, simple and sombre, but illuminated by the curé's conviction of ultimate grace, has a shape and direction which identify it as the plot of a well constructed novel. To retell it in this fashion, however, is to distort in two ways the actual experience of reading the book. First, it imposes an external perspective on a story told from within. Second, it glosses over the text's fragmentary nature. The reader can only arrive at such a summary by adopting an active role in piecing together a continuous narrative from the separate fragments which in reality constitute the book. It is the reader, not the writer – whether we think of the latter for the moment as the curé or Bernanos – who has shaped this coherent summary. And having done so, he will probably realise that an important ingredient is missing: the story of the writing of the diary itself. For one of the most pervasive images created by reading this novel is that of the curé struggling to confide his often anguished thoughts to paper. This mental picture is created partly through the explicit references to the act of writing and to the circumstances in which it takes place – the time of day or night, or his surroundings in Mme Duplouy's cafe in the final part, in an environment similar to that in which the novel was actually written; or his frame of mind, often affected by fatigue, depression or illness – and partly from the nature of the diary entries themselves: their alternation of short, tortured fragments and longer, more reflective passages of meditation and dialogue. This is not only a novel in diary form; it is also a novel about the writing of a diary: form and content are interdependent in a text with two distinct levels of narrative, which we can call, to borrow terms from the critical writings of Gérard Genette, the 'intradiegetic' narrative of the events recorded by the curé and the 'extradiegetic' narrative of their setting down on paper.

(ii) Time and typography

The degree to which first-time readers are aware that they are reading a diary and not just a standard novel can depend greatly on which edition they have chosen, or chanced, to read. This is because the typographical presentation of the diary entries varies considerably from one version of the text to another. In all editions of the novel, the text is divided into sections of greatly varying length, from a single line to over thirty pages, by a series of more or less long blank spaces, sometimes reinforced by a single or double dotted line. In several recent editions, including the popular Livre de poche (1970) and Pocket (1984) editions as well as the London University Press text of 1969, the spaces are relatively compressed, and attention is not drawn to them, so that it is quite possible for an unwary reader to miss their significance, and to read through them as if the entire text, apart from its division into three parts, were a continuous piece of prose. The effect of this can be the virtual disappearance from the reader's consciousness of the important extradiegetic level of narrative, resulting in an inability to share with the fictional diarist the agonies of writing and the existential awareness of passing time – vital elements of a successful reading of the novel. Bernanos, in truth, helped neither his editors nor his readers in this respect. His manuscript, which is now located in the Bibliothèque Nationale in Paris, is simply divided into unmarked paragraphs, separated by one or, more rarely, two blank lines; the dotted lines familiar to readers of the printed text were used by him only in sequences relating the curé's mental turmoil, where they indicate the fragmentary nature of his self-possession. While the *Revue hebdomadaire* version uses asterisks as dividers in some of its instalments, the sections thus created often do not correspond to those in either the manuscript or later printed editions. It is clear that Bernanos, in his intense concentration on the substance of his text, characteristically left to others the question of its lay-out. His first editors, Plon, divided the novel into sections introduced by a triple diamond – a strategy copied by some later editions, like those of the Imprimerie Nationale (1951), Atlantica Editoria (Rio, 1944), Plon (1957) and the Pléiade volume of the complete novels (1980). In all these versions, there are 59 sections: six in the first part, 52 in the long central part, and a single thirty-page section forming the final part of the text except for Dufréty's last-page letter to the curé de Torcy. This division has been criticised by some as arbitrary and unhelpful. As stated above, it rests on no authentic authorial sanction. Nor does it resolve in any way one of the greatest enigmas of *Journal d'un curé de campagne*: namely, the precise passage of time between the individual entries in the fictional but supposedly real diary of the young priest.

In common experience, keepers of diaries date each entry as part of the chronological record of experience which is one of the main impulses behind such writing. Equally traditionally, writers of novels, especially those with a pretension to realism, have shown a strong preoccupation with the plotting of events in time: scarcely one important action in Balzac's novels is not set in a very definite historical moment, fixed by reference to calendar and clock. If ever a text might have been expected to orient itself by clear chronological signposts, it would be a fictional diary by a writer for whom Balzac's *Comédie humaine* had been one of the great formative works of his early reading. Thus it comes as a surprise for the new reader of Bernanos's novel to find the fragments undated – except for the last fragment of all, Dufréty's letter, which is tantalisingly headed 'Lille, le ... février 19...' The idea of dating the diary entries apparently occurred to Bernanos, or else to his editors, for it was implemented in the second instalment of the *Revue hebdomadaire* text, the eight sections of which are given dates from November 17th to December 11th. This was an experiment which was quickly abandoned, perhaps wisely, for had these dates survived into the final published novel, the fact that they conflict with the date on which the curé begins to write his diary – November 25th, as indicated in the opening part (p.1035/34) – would have exacerbated the chronological difficulties even further. These discrepancies perhaps suggest Bernanos's incorrigible incapacity for the management of such details or perhaps his indifference to them. From the evidence of his published correspondence, in which a majority of his own letters are vaguely dated at best, and sometimes not at all, their dates having been reconstituted by their editors, one might speculate that precise dates were alien to his impatient temperament. More profoundly, it is possible that he shared the view of the curé de Torcy that 'le temps n'est rien pour le bon Dieu, son regard passe au travers' (p.1186/221).

A fairly clear overall time scheme embracing the main events of the novel is nevertheless distinguishable. We know when the curé begins to write his diary, and that he intends to burn it on November 25th of the following year, twelve months from its starting date (p.1035/34). We also know from the date of Dufréty's letter to Torcy that the curé dies in February. The precise moment of his death is also easily calculated: his appointment with the doctor in Lille is fixed for the 15th of the month (p.1208/247), and he dies, Dufréty says, shortly after four o'clock the following morning (p.1259/312). The final fragments of the diary are headed 'Minuit, chez M. Dufréty' (p.1242/292), and towards their end the curé remarks that dawn cannot be far away, as the sound of milkmen's carts confirms just before his final collapse (p.1256/309). From these details we can infer that the composition of the diary occupies eighty-four days, inclusive, from November 25th to the small hours of February 16th. Obviously, the fifty-nine sections of the Plon or Pléiade texts referred to above do not match this 84-day period of composition. Any attempt to read them as if each represented a consecutive daily entry would be misguided, and would soon founder on the rocks of conflicting textual detail. Some of the sections include paragraphs which are explicitly written at a later date than the preceding portion of the same section. Examples include the indication of a two-day long reflection after a visit to Dr Delbende, which has just been narrated (p.1096/110), and a clearly marked interval of two days in the middle of a long and complex sequence in Part Two (p.1195/232) – a sequence which has a further implied gap during which the curé goes to bed and resumes writing the following morning (p.1201/239). Likewise, a night has explicitly elapsed between his final visit to the countess and the news of her death, which reaches him at 6.30 the next morning, although both are recorded in the same section (p.1166/196). As well as these lapses of time within single sections of text, there are also implied intervals between sections. That two days have elapsed between Chantal's two visits to the curé – narrated in consecutive entries – is indicated by his description of her face, on her second visit, as 'encore plus torturé qu'*avant-hier* (p.1132/154, my emphasis). The Pléiade divisions sometimes correspond to the events of a single day, and reading them successively sometimes corresponds to the passing from one day to the next, but often neither of these is the case, and on such occasions the editors seem to have been more interested in bracketing passages that form a thematic rather than temporal unity. This leads them at times to include, within one single starred section, separate paragraphs which indicate that the curé has stopped writing and resumed his text later to augment or comment on the interrupted sequence of writing. The Pléiade divisions are thus certainly not arbitrary, but neither do they correspond to precise moments of time. Indeed, the sequences of composition of the diary are of a complexity which no existing edition, by its typographical lay-out alone, can fully represent.

It is clear that the curé, despite his initial decision to maintain a regular daily record 'au jour le jour' (p.1036/35), his references to the comfort obtained from writing 'matin et soir' (p.1171/202), and his declared inability to leave his diary behind him during the anticipated one-day absence in Lille (p.1223/266), does not write every day. Conversely, there are some days on which he writes several times, notably the fateful day in Lille, punctuated by bursts of writing in Mme Duplouy's cafe and in Dufréty's apartment. Elisabeth Lagadec-Sadoulet, in the most rigorous attempt so far to reconstitute a chronology of the diary's composition, is surely correct to identify 'moments d'écriture', of which she counts ninety-eight (*34*, p.102), as the true units of its extradiegetic time. But even her intricate calculations do not yield a precise calendar of events, as she readily admits. Indeed, any attempt to produce a micro-chronology aimed at embracing every detail down to the days of the week would be thwarted not just by a lack of precise indicators of time, but also by what look like errors on Bernanos's part. The curé, for example, is invited to lunch at the château 'mardi prochain' (p.1052/57); a day which transforms itself, five pages later, into a Saturday, making any earnest counting of intervening fragments futile. A similar problem arises from the expected arrival of the housekeeper Mme Pégriot. We are informed that it is due to take place on a Tuesday (p.1053/57); thus, to be consistent, the curé's record, written on the day after the good lady's visit, has to be written on a Wednesday – but if this is so, it implies an interval, for which there is no other evidence, of over a week since his attendance at the curé d'Hébertune's lecture on *another* Tuesday (p.1054/59). Subtle calculations of days backwards or forwards from fragments which describe the curé's catechism classes, based on the probability that these take place on their traditional Thursday, likewise stumble on improbabilities – such as the apparent delivery of mail on Sunday. Even greater feats of zeal on the part of the village postman would be needed to account for the seemingly instant arrival of replies to the curé's letters to Dufréty and to the doctor in Lille. The attentive reader will in fact find no shortage of temporal contradictions, such as the mismatch between the beginning and the end of the recording of the visit to the presbytery by the chanoine de la Motte-Beuvron (pp.1171-75/203-07). This passage begins with the latter's departure, apparently leaving the curé alone and about to write up their conversation, but ends with the curé leaving the house with his visitor and then, when he resumes writing, recording the later visit of the count instead.

Further analysis of the chronological unclarities of the text would be tedious. The essential point is that it is impossible to regard the novel as a convincingly realistic representation of a genuine diary. Even the more obvious questions – in which year does the action take place? where has Christmas disappeared to in the course of the passage of time from November to February? – cannot be answered, except perhaps in the most general or symbolic terms. The background of the action, broadly speaking, is that of the financially depressed 1930s, as is evidenced by a reference to the 'terrible Crise' (p.1081/92) which historically arose from the financial crash of 1929. There seems no reason not to suppose that the novel's fictional time corresponds to the 'real' time in which Bernanos wrote it: the mid-1930s. As for Christmas, this is a feast of particular significance in the earlier novel *Sous le soleil de Satan*, which takes the birthday of the Christ-child as its chronological starting-point and associates it with the identification of the special mission of the novel's hero, the abbé Donissan, but the curé d'Ambricourt, designated 'de toute éternité' as 'prisonnier de la Sainte Agonie' (p.1187/222), is marked instead by the stigmata of the Passion and thus associated with the first Easter – so that Christmas, quite possibly, is for him a strange irrelevance. He would, in this respect, be the precursor and spiritual brother of Sœur Blanche de la Sainte-Agonie, the heroine of Bernanos's final literary work *Dialogues des Carmélites*. It is tempting, if one wishes to pursue the notion of christic symbolism, to imagine that the curé's death occurs on a Friday morning, on a symbolic anniversary of the Crucifixion. This is a hypothesis, however, to which the text lends no support, although one might notice that the only year in the entire 1930s decade in which February 16th fell on a Friday was 1934, the year in which the novel was begun: whether this is coincidence or not is a question which nobody can answer. The fact that in the manuscript Dufréty's letter is dated February 7th just serves to make the problem even less soluble.

One has to conclude that Bernanos was not trying to construct a chronologically perfect diary. The novelist was writing a novel. This was a priority which made it important to achieve a freedom from mechanical concerns with dating. Perhaps, remembering other

novels, such as *Monsieur Ouine*, of which the chronology is
notoriously unclear, a wise conclusion might be that Bernanos's often
uncertain recording of time is simply a characteristic of his art,
conscious or unconscious, and adds to the mystery and fascination of
his text. But he was also clearly seeking, as a novelist intent on
persuading his reader of the fictional reality of the text, to create at
least the general illusion of a diary. Because of this, the divisions of
the Pléiade edition, of an average length of under four pages, but
with nearly a third of them less than one page long and only six
running to more than ten pages, are valuable, whether Bernanos
authorised them or not, in producing an effect of fragmentation
which a more continuous lay-out can conceal. However generally and
imprecisely, they create the *impression* of a diary, which was
probably the author's minimal intention. It is for this reason that the
writer of this guide passes on to its readers the advice given as a
practising university teacher to a generation of students: either to
work from the Pléiade edition or else to pencil the divisions of its
text into their cheaper paperback editions, of which the current
Pocket edition is the most easily available.

(iii) The novelist in the diary

If the pretext of the diary cannot be totally sustained without
granting Bernanos a liberal novelist's licence, the presence in the
diary of the novelist's controlling hand needs little proving. The
division of the text into three numbered chapters, albeit of greatly
varying length, gives it, to begin with, the external shape of a three-
part novel. These divisions, self-evidently, are not made by the curé
himself. Pragmatically, we know they result from decisions made by
the novelist and/or his publisher – probably the latter, as the original
manuscript is not divided in this way. But in addition to these
extraneous textual organisers, another editor, whom we must regard
as fictional because he exists within the text, can also be seen at
work. It is he who informs us that a certain phrase has been added in
the margin of the diary and then crossed out (p.1145/170), or that
several pages have been ripped out of the curé's manuscript, that

some marginal scribbles are illegible, that some crossings-out have
been affected with such force as to tear holes in the paper
(p.1184/218), and that a certain sentence has been left unfinished and
is followed by an unknown number of missing lines, thus leaving him
with no option but to present the curé's final conversation with Torcy
as he found it, with its opening lost for ever (p.1185/219). This
'implied' editor, in an italicised aside, even expresses a subjective
opinion on the manner in which pages have been removed – '*en hâte
semble-t-il*' (p.1184/218). Such devices, obviously, are part of a
trompe-l'œil strategy to win the reader's connivance with the diary's
reality, and they have their element of convention as well as of
artifice. Missing pages are similarly commented upon by an alleged
editor in Jean-Paul Sartre's later novel *La Nausée*, which similarly
includes suggestions that the mental turmoil of the diarist explains
the ferocity with which he has destroyed parts of his text.
Conventional also is the device, made necessary by the curé's death
in the act of writing, of having Dufréty provide the novel's formal
ending, in the shape of his letter to Torcy recording his former
friend's last moments; François Mauriac had already employed the
technique, to deal with similar narrative circumstances, at the end of
Le Nœud de vipères. Whether these additions to the curé's text are
made by Dufréty, who would then emerge as its editor, is unclear but
improbable. The diary must logically have fallen into his hands
because the curé is writing it up to the moment of death in Dufréty's
flat. But the signs are that Dufréty, who is a would-be writer, has
chosen not to reveal to Torcy or anyone else the diary's existence. He
provides Torcy with mere 'renseignements' (p.1258/311) on the
events of February 16th, adding that he intends to complete, if his
health allows, a fuller account which he hopes to publish in a local
journal. This implies that Dufréty, far from merely preparing the
diary for its own authentic publication, is busily plagiarising it for his
own profit. The question of the diary's ultimate fate, like a number of
other questions in this novel, remains unresolved. Logically, we
could not read it if had not been preserved. But, more pragmatically
still, substituting our own reality as readers of the book for that of
companions of the curé, we read his diary as if we were looking over

his shoulder as he writes. Our willing acceptance of this relationship
with the text is a form of 'suspension of disbelief', a complicity with
the narrative which is probably the only demand which Bernanos
would make of us. Each of us becomes in fact the 'implied reader', of
whose presence both the novelist and the fictional author are
conscious as they write.

As such, we are privy to things which even the curé cannot see,
or at least cannot record, notably the symbolic significance of
apparently trivial events. One of the most impressive features of the
novel is the way in which, while working wholly from within the
curé's verbal reconstruction of experience, the novelist is able to
suggest ideas that lie beyond his conscious thoughts. The curé's
enforced diet of bread and wine, for example, is to him merely the
natural consequence of his poor physical health, but the reader is led
by the novelist to see it as a perpetual Eucharist. Further liturgical or
traditional Catholic symbolism is implied in the scene in which
Séraphita wipes the face of the fallen curé in re-enactment of the
ministrations of Saint Veronica to the stricken Christ (p.1200/238). It
is important that the curé should remain unaware of these parallels
for both psychological and literary reasons. Too conscious an
imitation of Christ would preserve neither his humility nor the
novel's status as a text free of heavy allegory.

A fine example of Bernanos's art of investing deep significance
into seemingly chance detail by juxtaposing and interrelating the
curé's diary entries occurs in the brief narration of the visit to the
sacristy of the little orphan boy Sylvestre Galuchet. Neglected and
dirty, brought up after his mother's death by an alcoholic
grandmother but nevertheless the best pupil in the curé's catechism
class, Sylvestre exudes 'une innocence d'avant le péché, une
innocente pureté d'animal pur' (p.1100/115). These words create a
contrastive echo of the earlier account of the curé's difficulties in
communicating with the village children, whose observation of
animals has given them an inevitable early insight into sexual
realities (p.1051/55). More immediately, the boy's visit, narrated at
the end of a section describing a 'nuit affreuse' of depression, brings
to the curé 'cette pitié que j'attendais' (p.1100/115). Sylvestre, it is

made clear to us by the novelist's prompting, does not just happen to call, despite the acceptable pretext of his wish to collect a pious image awarded for his good work. By implication, although once more the curé must not see this, Sylvestre's coming represents an act of God's mercy. It is also a typical event in novels by Bernanos, in which nothing 'just happens'. A real-life diary, that supreme vehicle for the recording of the genuinely trivial, arguably obscures the patterns within and behind life's events, including the patterns which a Christian might identify as providential. The curé's fictitious diary, in which nothing is trivial, in which all that occurs is articulated into significance by textual ordering, is in this sense a kind of 'anti-diary'. It is a novel which challenges and transcends the format of the diary in which it ultimately only pretends to be cast. And in the parallels it suggests between the consciously shaping devices of the novelist and the invisible hand of God behind the complex rhythms of life, it becomes a powerful mode of expression, in its very form, of Bernanos's Christian conception of the human condition.

(iv) The curé and his diary

The diary, as well as providing the novelist with the external form of his text, is also important within the book's internal structure through the role it plays in the life of the central character. The curé initially regards the keeping of a diary as a strictly controlled experiment, to last a mere twelvemonth. This resolution is not realised, not only because of his death in February but more crucially still because he changes his mind, and expresses a new resolution to 'ne pas détruire ce journal' (pp.1184/218-19). It quickly becomes precious to him as a 'trésor caché' (p.1223/266) from which he can never part. In his continuing torment, the diary is his mainstay. When the suspicion of blame hangs over him after the countess's death, he writes: 'Il semble donc que j'aurais mieux à faire que d'écrire ces lignes. Et cependant j'ai plus que jamais besoin de ce journal' (p.1171/202). When he takes it with him to Lille, unable to leave it behind even for a day or two, he is driven obsessively to write at the table in Mme Duplouy's café, recording not just the immediate pain of the sentence of death passed on him by the doctor, but the refreshing memories of early mornings, the cries of cocks in the pure light of dawn: 'Mon Dieu, il faut que je l'écrive...' (p.1231/278).

The aims and rewards of this writing are questions to which he obsessively returns, and three interconnected functions of the diary emerge. The first is to 'voir clair en moi' (p.1171/202): to clarify his own inner thoughts and feelings. The diary offers him 'un témoignage très précieux, [...] assez précis pour fixer ma pensée. Elles [its pages] m'ont délivré du rêve' (p.1223/267). Without this means of stabilising his ever-fleeing emotions by anchoring them in the relative fixity of words, he is prone to the nightmarish torments of 'on ne sait quelle rêverie vague, informe', of 'un demi-sommeil qui trouble toutes les perspectives du souvenir, fait de chacune de mes journées écoulées un paysage de brumes, sans repères, sans routes' (p.1171/202). His diary fills this sense of spatial solitude. Second, it compensates for the absence from his life of regular human companionship. Before his decision to write, the act of reading had already brought him the joy of communing with other minds: the autobiography of Maxim Gorky in particular had awakened his sympathies for the oppressed masses of Tsarist Russia and had given him 'tout un peuple pour compagnon' (p.1070/79). This communion through reading is complemented by writing. As he writes, the curé is increasingly conscious of 'une présence invisible qui n'est sûrement pas celle de Dieu – plutôt d'un ami fait à mon image, bien que distinct de moi, d'une autre essence' (p.1049/51), '[un] auditeur imaginaire', whose image crystallises later into that of the 'futur lecteur, probablement imaginaire, de ce journal' (p.1117/136): it is an image of us, of each individual reader of the text, drawn into the intimacy of the curé's heart. Third, the diary is consciously intended as an additional means of communication with God: 'une conversation entre le bon Dieu et moi, un prolongement de la prière' (p.1048/50). He often finds prayer difficult, partly because of the severity of the stomach pains which he has not identified as the symptoms of cancer, and partly because of the periods of spiritual alienation in which God seems silent. Even on his last full day on earth, after learning of the imminence of his death, the curé returns from a church, which he had found simply 'froide et noire', and where 'ce que j'attendais n'est pas venu' (p.1231/278), to the table at Mme Duplouy's, where his diary unfailingly awaits him.

The diary's role in his life, however, is not seen by all readers as a wholly positive one. To Gérard Hoffbeck, it locks the curé within a prison of misleading words and creates around him a series of distorting mirrors of the self, to such an extent, concludes Hoffbeck, that 'il ne faut sans doute pas chercher ailleurs la cause de la nuit intérieure que vit le prêtre' (*14*, p.80). This analysis appears, to the writer of this present guide, ill founded. The curé's determination, despite his original intention, not to destroy his diary stems ultimately from his realisation that it sustains him, and that he must thus sustain it. This is seen most clearly when, having torn out a number of pages in which he has apparently recorded a powerful urge to take his own life, he nevertheless restores to his mutilated text, in briefer form, a confession of the temptation to commit what for a Catholic, and a Catholic priest to boot, is a mortal sin. He writes:

> Résolu que je suis a ne pas détruire ce journal, mais ayant cru devoir faire disparaître ces pages écrites dans un véritable délire, je veux néanmoins porter contre moi ce témoignage que ma dure épreuve [...] m'a trouvé un moment sans résignation, sans courage, et que la tentation m'est venue de... (pp.1184-85/218-19)

The diary, far from obscuring truth behind a veil of words, is revealed here as the repository of the most hurtful of all truths, and as an extension of the sacrament of confession. This is not to say that writing cannot be subject to corruption and abuse, as is suggested through the second writer figure in the novel, Dufréty. The curé himself discerns such dangers. 'Tel quel,' he writes, 'ce journal tient-il trop de place dans ma vie... je l'ignore. Dieu le sait' (p.1171/202). And he admits that there may be 'quelque chose de maladif dans l'attachement que je porte à ces feuilles' (pp.1223/266-67). It is these expressions of anxiety which Hoffbeck registers, but then seems to draw from them a conclusion which ignores the significance of the opposition of the good and bad writer, exemplified by the curé/Dufréty duo.

The curé answers his own occasional misgivings about the writer's powers of distortion through selection, his calculation of the image which he wishes to project to the reader. He comments that secular writers – '[les] enfants du siècle' (p.1034/33) – take for granted that writing is a legitimate form of creating and re-creating the self, while the Christian knows that the self has to be accepted because given by God, and that 'On ne joue pas contre Dieu' (p.1034/33). It follows from this that his aim in writing must be 'cette connaissance surnaturelle de soi-même, de soi-même en Dieu, qui s'appelle la foi' (p.1129/150). Writing is a secondary form of confession and of prayer, testimony to the faith that resides within him but which he often has difficulty in locating. The diary becomes his only means to clear self-reflexion, the only source of recorded memory, the only focus of concentration to draw him out of futile dreaming, the only signpost in a landscape without landmarks or roads. His fear of his diary evaporates. In the end God will judge whether it has become too important. All he can do is keep it, 'scrupuleusement' and with a 'franchise absolue', 'une rigueur inflexible' (p.1036/35). This urge to truth must come from him; the diary repays him for this effort. Such is the contract between the curé and his diary, between the writer and his text.

2. The Curé and his World

(i) A typical parish

The opening words of the novel, 'Ma paroisse est une paroisse comme les autres' (p.1031/29), identify Ambricourt as a place with nothing to distinguish it from the multitude of France's rural parishes. Its ordinariness reflects the modest character of the priest whose mission is to serve it, for the site of his vocation can hardly inspire delusions of grandeur, let alone aspirations to saintliness. His first words also reinforce the intentions which Bernanos expressed to Vallery-Radot when the novel was in its planning phase: 'Je voudrais aussi que ce petit village fût un "condensé" de notre pays – le châtelain, l'adjoint, l'épicier, les gosses, je les vois tous'(8, II, p.48). Bernanos espouses here the ambition of a Realist writer: the creation of a world which, while imaginary, holds up a mirror to the real world outside literature. His 'seeing' these details, through the eye of imagination but corroborating that vision by reference to the eyes of the flesh, is also a characteristic of the Realist's aim: what one of Zola's characters, the painter Claude Lantier in L'Œuvre, describes as 'tout voir et tout peindre'. And, also like the great Realist novelists, he subscribes, at least provisionally, to an aesthetic of the ordinary and the average. The resemblance of Ambricourt to all other parishes makes it not just ordinary, but also typical – and through its typicality, extraordinary in its power of representation of the French rural world at large. Bernanos illustrates here the paradox of the Realist mode of fiction which by its exemplary completeness achieves the status of the symbolic. What Balzac said of literary characters – 'Tout personnage typique devient colossal par ce seul fait' – is true also of places.

Ambricourt represents any parish and all parishes because, the curé remarks in his second sentence, 'Toutes les paroisses se ressemblent', only to add, importantly: 'Les paroisses d'aujourd'hui, naturellement.' This is another early indication of how we should read this text, namely, with a consciousness of historical perspective. Christendom was once different, the curé's afterthought implies; his parish is representative of the modern parish, and of modern Christendom. Other characters in the book may espouse a more static view of the world and of the Church's place within it. Not so the curé, who is aware of change and of the need for institutions, including the Church, to adapt to it.

These social and religious ideas form a major part of the novel's interest. Although the world it reflects existed sixty years ago, the concerns it inspired in Bernanos – the decline in moral and spiritual values, the relationship between rich and poor, the conflicts between the various political responses to these questions – are still of the utmost relevance today. It is true that the options for 1930s France were clearer and starker than the plurality of routes that beckons our world of the 1990s, but the reminder of the moral implications of choosing between them has lost none of its urgency. The Fascist dictatorships established in two of France's neighbour countries, Italy and Germany, and with a Spanish version literally taking shape around Bernanos as he sat writing the novel in Palma, offered one model of social organisation, attractive to many of his former associates within the authoritarian Action Française. The Marxist-Leninist model of Soviet Russia offered another, the strong temptation of which in the eyes of a depressed proletariat is understood by the curé. During the later stages of the novel's composition, a left-wing Popular Front government came to power in France and instituted the most serious programme of social welfare ever seen in that country; its equivalent and forerunner, the Frente Popular government in Spain, was at the same time in the process of being crushed by Franco's rebellion. Drawn in one direction by political affiliation and in the other by compassion for the poor, Bernanos was acutely aware of a need for fresh thinking and of a lack of leadership and commitment within the Church and in its ranks of traditional supporters.

His novels habitually allude to such political issues, but in indirect ways. He once described *Sous le soleil de Satan* as a response to the demonic slaughter of the Great War, and *Nouvelle histoire de Mouchette* as a novel inspired by the fratricidal conflict in Spain, although war and politics are not specifically mentioned in either but are reflected at the deeper level of moral or theological theme. It is necessary to read the *Journal* in the same way, with an awareness of background and a sensitivity to thematic connections between its different levels. There are two focal points to consider in studying its social and political dimensions: the microcosm of the particular parish in which these issues are exemplified and the macrocosm of the wider world to which they relate symbolically and through the magnifying glass of their typicality.

(ii) The curé and his parish

The *Nouveau Petit Larousse* defines 'paroisse' as 'territoire sur lequel s'étend la juridiction spirituelle d'un curé'; and 'curé' is defined by the *Petit Robert* as 'prêtre placé à la tête d'une paroisse'. A parish is both a geographical and spiritual space, and the curé's leadership of it is inscribed in the constitution of the Church. In the novel's opening lines this relationship is underlined by almost incantatory repetition. In the first three paragraphs, 'paroisse' occurs eight times, and the associated noun 'village' four times. To these twelve verbal signifiers of the territory of Ambricourt, there correspond (ignoring the intercalated conversation with the curé de Norenfontes) thirteen first-person indicators ('je', 'me', 'mon/ma', 'mienne') which identify the diarist as its guardian and protector. This near-perfect lexical balance thrusts priest and parish, together and in equal proportions, to the forefront of the text in a symbiotic relationship grounded in its verbal substance. It is there again in an echoing passage twenty pages later when, on the 'anniversary' (three months, to be precise) of his arrival in Ambricourt, the curé views the village from the same vantage point and confesses that he cannot utter the word 'paroisse' without emotion. The noun is used four more times, each time with the adjective 'ma', again underpinning grammatically his conviction that 'nous sommes l'un à l'autre pour l'éternité' (p.1052/56).

The village, when first seen, appears passive and indifferent. The curé describes it as a tired cow, steaming in the late autumn rain, then disappearing into the night. To this image of the wandering beast there corresponds that of the 'petit vacher' (p.1031/30), whom he imagines coming home from school and leading the herd to its warm stable. The 'maître à suivre' required by the morally lost herd/parish must possess the childlike qualities of the little schoolboy/cowherd. The novelist already prompts the reader to realise that, just as the parish is the archetype of all parishes, the curé is the archetype of the saviour, identified metaphorically as the little cowherd, and symbolically as a Christ figure. A saint, writes the diarist, is required to save this village, but his own fitness for that role remains unformulated.

The second passage refers to the village's 'regard' or way of looking at him, which he describes as the 'regard' of Christendom, or of the entire human race, searching imploringly for a guide. The image bites deep into his imagination; he uses it in a sermon, to his own embarrassment, for nobody understands. And when he tries once more, a few pages later, to catch its 'regard' from his favourite hill-top, the village also fails to respond. Yet he is conscious still of a latent sign of recognition: 'Je ne crois pas d'ailleurs non plus qu'il m'ignore. On dirait qu'il me tourne le dos et m'observe de biais, les yeux mi-clos, à la manière des chats. Que me veut-il? Me veut-il même quelque chose?' (pp.1060-61/67). Again the novelist's prompting answers the diarist's question – what the village will want of the curé is Christ-like suffering on its behalf. For the young priest, we are told, sometimes imagines himself nailed to a cross by the village and watched, as he dies, by its piercing look.

Such thoughts are alien to the people of Ambricourt. The 'village' does not behave as a 'paroisse' in the spiritual sense, and not once do we see its inhabitants acting together in the practice of their supposed faith. On the contrary: they project a reverse image of a Christian community, a negative that is tantamount to a picture of evil. The curé does not leap immediately into such theological areas of vocabulary, but rather diagnoses the condition of the villagers as one of 'ennui' (pp.1031-32/30). By this word he obviously means something more profound than its dictionary sense of 'boredom'. Readers of Baudelaire will register Bernanos's probably conscious echo of his use of the word to signify a pervasive world-weariness and self-disgust. The curé defines it as a kind of devouring cancer or leprosy, spreading slowly and contagiously through the world. It is a deep-grained despair, an absence of the Christian virtue of hope, a symbol of the 'christianisme décomposé' (p.1032/31) which is the essence of our secularised society. The curé regards his parishioners as the passive victims of this corruption. It is part of the air they breathe, coating their bodies and invading their lungs like an invisible dust. Exposure to it is the perpetual condition of life in the modern world.

The curé sees the villagers as victims rather than perpetrators of evil. They include rapacious merchants like M. Pamyre, who dupes him out of his meagre resources (p.1035/54), or the local schoolmaster who sells patent drugs as a sideline and is offended by the curé's well-meaning free distribution of medicines which he happens to receive from an old seminary friend (p.1110/127). These may appear trivial examples of the suffering of a socially awkward individual in a hard economic world. Less trivial are the signs of a deep-rooted hostility towards him among the villagers, manifested by attempts to interrupt his sleep, and culminating in anonymous letters advising him to leave (pp.1111/127-28). Such persecution, accompanied by a reputation for alcoholism created by his growing consumption of wine – the only beverage he can tolerate as his abdominal pains increase – is incomprehensible to the curé; this rejection of God's representative amounts to a hatred of God Himself, so evil that he thinks it must be of diabolical origin: 'La haine de Dieu me fait toujours penser à la possession...' (p.1105/121).

Even the young people of Ambricourt have been contaminated by this all-pervading spiritual sickness. The curé seeks shelter in his catechism classes, hoping they will bring him closer to the children for whom, remembering Christ's words 'Sinite parvulos' ('Except ye

[...] become as little children...', Matthew 18. 3), he feels a special tenderness. But the children too are already versed in the ways of the world, and respond with smutty-minded resistance to his teachings on spiritual love. The peasant girl Séraphita Dumouchel for whom he feels particular compassion shows a talent for precocious sexual teasing. More compromising for the curé is his attempt to befriend the young house-painter Sulpice Mitonnet, in whom he naïvely fails to detect a sexual ambivalence which causes the other youths to boycott him.

These encounters with the economic and sexual realities of the world's corruption are aggravated by evidence of its loss of Christian belief. This is expressed not by an intellectual character but by a simple man in whom the curé had expected to find the old beliefs intact: the gravedigger Arsène, who declares that he does not believe in conversion or even in resurrection: 'Quand on est mort, tout est mort' (p.1182/216). The curé reassures himself that Arsène, who works for the Church and regards himself as a member of its body, no doubt does believe in eternity, albeit unthinkingly. But he is shaken by this glimpse of the scepticism that lies within an allegedly Christian community.

The family of the count and countess sets no better example, although exemplary behaviour is precisely what the curé expects from these traditional allies of the Church. Bernanos expresses nostalgia here for the ideals of a pre-industrial feudal society, in which the local lord's God-given authority over his peasant tenants was accorded on the condition of his reciprocal care and guidance of them. That such ideals no longer correspond to modern reality is a lesson which the curé learns only gradually. He awaits his first visit to the château in anticipation and is even flattered to be invited, for his simple, passively resigned background has left him with no jealousy or resentment of the rich. The count, he comments, 'ressemble certainement plus à un paysan comme moi qu'à n'importe quel riche industriel', and even the mantilla of the countess 'm'a rappelé celle que ma pauvre maman mettait le dimanche...' (p.1059/65). He is charmed by their naturalness and elegance, and more at ease in their company than in that of the 'anciens minotiers' who have recently bought a neighbouring château. Yet the count's values are later revealed as no less material than theirs. As the chanoine de la Motte-Beuvron tells the curé, 'Il n'y a plus de nobles, mon cher ami, mettez-vous cela dans la tête. [...] Les nobles d'aujourd'hui sont des bourgeois honteux' (pp.1174-75/206-07). Far from leading his community, the count is revealed in all his mediocrity as a man responsible for the fragmentation of his own family through his affair with the governess Mlle Louise, which is pushing his daughter Chantal towards flight or even suicide. 'On devrait beaucoup prier pour les familles,' he tells the curé (p.1175/208): this great central institution, bulwark of traditional values, is in no less danger of collapse than other ancient institutions of France.

Among these threatened guardians of values is the Church itself, and again the fault lies within. It would be a mistake to imagine that Bernanos, fervent Catholic though he was, assumed an automatically defensive position with regard to his Church. Indeed, in his eyes the modern Church had betrayed the mission confided in it, and his assessment of the attitudes of its hierarchy is so critical that it would not be excessive to define it as a form of anticlericalism. Against the tide of the institution's failure, however, swim various 'bons prêtres'. The first of these, mentioned only once, is the curé de Norenfontes, 'très bienveillant, très paternel', but also, significantly, with a reputation in the archbishop's circle of being 'un esprit fort, un peu dangereux' (p.1031/29). He seems to be an *alter ego* of the curé de Torcy or, not impossibly, simply an early version of Torcy, introduced and then forgotten during textual redraftings. Torcy too had once been the priest at Norenfontes (p.1075/85); and like him, this man bears the traces of suffering and fatigue which move the curé almost to tears. Brief though his appearance is, he is the first of the curé's soul-brothers, an early sign of his need for human solidarity and warmth, his capacity for emotional involvement.

His superiors, certainly, provide none of this solace. Individual priests are not encouraged to have their own views, but are advised to emulate the quietude of the monk. This indoctrination is dispensed through lectures which the curé attends, reluctantly and at the command of his *doyen*, but which he finds pointless and irrelevant. One is delivered by the archiprêtre de Bailloeil, '[un] ancien professeur de lettres [qui] soigne sa diction comme ses mains', a typical example of 'le prêtre lettré [qui] m'a toujours fait horreur' (pp.1033-34/32). The lecture is on 'Ce que j'ai vu à Verchocq', but the curé is sceptical of the interest of what can be seen in that monastery or any other. Whereas earlier Catholic novelists like Huysmans or Léon Bloy had been so moved by the spectacle of monastic life as to situate large sections of their novels in such environments, Bernanos was obviously of the opinion that exemplary piety is easier to achieve in the cloister than in the hurly-burly world of the parish. His novel reflects here the age-long tension within the Church between regular and secular clergy; but it also indicates his own greater interest in a setting where religious and social concerns can be explored in their direct interrelationship.

As for the second lecture attended by the curé, on the schisms of the Church in the sixteenth century, he is sensitive to its relevance to the problematic issue of the Church's twentieth-century survival. The other priests, less imbued with Bernanos's historical sense, are oblivious to this. What they understand are matters of which the curé is wholly ignorant: financial realities into which, as the son of poor peasants, he has never been initiated. The Church's institutional concern with money, and its complicity with the world of commerce, are represented by a further priest, the rebarbative doyen de Blangermont who, reproaching the curé for his unpaid debts to the Pamyres, defends the latter as pillars of a social class 'qui fait encore la richesse et la grandeur de notre cher pays' (p.1081/92). The Church's alliance with the property-owning 'bourgeoisie travailleuse, épargnante', now threatened by 'les éléments de désordre', has for him a scriptural backing, for 'le droit de propriété n'est-il pas inscrit dans l'Evangile?' Property, wealth and order are clearly superior in this priest's scale of values to pastoral care or even to saintliness – for he protests unconvincingly that his cry 'Dieu nous préserve [...] des saints!' was a mere 'boutade' (p.1082/93).

A second highly ranked clergyman to represent a particular interest against the curé is the chanoine de la Motte-Beuvron, who, as the count's uncle, is concerned to protect the family name after the countess's sudden death. Although he has harsh words to say about his nephew he is careful to distance himself from the curé also. With impeccable correctness, he declares his wish to respect his young colleague's authority in his own parish, and he speaks to him 'sur un ton d'égal à égal, presque de déférence', but at the same time he assures him: '[qu'] il est probable que nous n'avons pas deux idées communes en ce qui touche le gouvernement des paroisses' (pp.1172-73/204). Thus, siding with no-one and standing back from all, his every sentence cancelling the one before, the unctuous canon shows that he belongs to the category of devious and unscrupulous career priests described by Bernanos in *L'Imposture*. He may feign respect for the curé, but he is also insistent, ecclesiastical civil servant that he is, that his young colleague should write down the details of his last encounter with the countess, to be shown to the bishop and then safely filed away within the bowels of the institution. This cold and efficient man is a telling portrait of the type of priest who sits comfortably aloof in the hierarchy of a Church whose true mission, Bernanos believes, is to involve itself in the everyday world and cure it of its cancer.

(iii) The macrocosm: the Church and the world

Collectively, these individual portraits of members of the parish and Church constitute a remarkably complete impression of a traditional society, divided into its classical 'three estates': aristocracy, priests and a multifarious 'tiers état' composed of merchants, artisans and peasant farmers. However, behind this apparent structural stability, old distinctions of class are fragmenting, the aristocracy has surrendered its central place to a commercial middle-class, itself pressurised by the financial crash of 1929, and in the background there are glimpses of a poor and deprived rural community. The role of the Church in this society has become unclear – as unclear, precisely, as the role of the curé in his parish, so that defining the one is the key to elucidating the other. This task of definition is the function of the long passages of discursive dialogue which account for about a fifth of the entire novel, and in which the central figures are the curé de Torcy, doctor Delbende and the countess's nephew Olivier Tréville-Sommerange.

Dialogue in general is a dominant component of all of Bernanos's novels, for most of their important scenes are dramatic two-person confrontations. The central 'countess scene', as well as the curé's conversations with the count, Chantal, Louise and, later, with Doctor Laville, Dufréty and Dufréty's mistress, are all examples of such 'dramatic' dialogues. One can distinguish from them the dialogues which amplify the themes noted above: the curé's five discussions with Torcy, and especially the two great dialogues early in the book (pp.1036-47/35-48, 1066-80/74-91); the brief but important exchange with Delbende (pp.1091-96/104-10); the longer one with Olivier near the end of the Ambricourt sequence of the novel (pp.1209-21/249-64). To label these as 'discursive' dialogues is not to imply that they are abstract essays that might have strayed into the novel from works of non-fiction. On the contrary, in reporting the discourse of his interlocutors, the curé reproduces the circumlocutions and frequent incoherence of their spontaneous utterances. He does not rephrase them in his own more analytical style, but allows the voices of the various speakers to be heard in their own idiom, as essential elements of their portraits. Bernanos, who makes his curé say: 'Je ne suis pas l'ambassadeur du Dieu des philosophes, je suis le serviteur de Jésus-Christ' (p.1096/110), is not 'philosophising', but putting into his characters' mouths half-formed thoughts on which the curé, often just listening in virtual silence, reflects and comments later. His meditations on these thoughts (pp.1047-48/48-50, 1061-66/68-74), linking the dialogues and carrying the chain of ideas forward as an integral part of the narrative, are the final components of a fugue of developing themes, important both as a commentary on the social situation underlying the narrative and as a clarification of the nature and significance of the curé's mission.

No summary in English can do justice to the rich language of the interlocutors, nor capture the teeming complexity of their ideas. Even their personalities are elusive. Henri Giordan argues that the curé de Torcy defies analysis: 'Bernanos y a introduit des éléments difficiles à concilier de prime abord' (*9* (d), p.98). This is no doubt because this sympathetic priest, described by Robert Speaight as Bernanos's nearest approach to a self-portrait (*42*, p.147), is caught in different moods in his various appearances. The curé's companion, self-imposed mentor and debating partner, he is sometimes carried away by the resonance of his own eloquence, at other moments moved to tears by his thoughts of human suffering. A man of courage, vigour, mock irreverence and humour – he is indeed the main provider of an attractively humorous dimension in the novel – he represents through his own character his conviction that Christianity exists to bring joy to the world. Yet Torcy's 'gros rire bonhomme' is also an ironic guard against too intimate a relationship with others, a trait which the curé finds disappointing. There is also a vulnerability in him, born of the conflicts with the Church hierarchy related in the second dialogue. The curé realises, observing Torcy's trembling hands as they discuss the Church's social role, the damage incurred in Torcy from the 'luttes terribles où avaient failli sombrer son courage, sa raison, sa foi peut-être' (p.1071/80). He seems to have emerged from these struggles as a tamer man, at least in public. While passionately declaiming his rebelliousness in the privacy of his room, there is little to suggest a continuing active role. Though far from being the self-seeking careerist priest, establishment flatterer or pretentious intellectual of the type from whom the curé recoils, the fact that Torcy is a possible candidate for the deanship of Heuchin (p.1036/35) suggests that he has exercised care in recent times not to be seen as a trouble-maker. He has the worldly wisdom which the curé lacks. There is even a suggestion that he leans towards the side of the villagers in their judgment of the curé, believing as they do that he is an alcoholic. Torcy also realises, however, his colleague's qualities and the special calling which awaits him.

Olivier and Delbende also offer the curé a fraternity based on shared values. Both, like him, have known rejection. Olivier's early reputation as 'un garçon très difficile' (p.1210/250) has made him a semi-outcast from the countess's family. With this soldier in the Foreign Legion, whose everyday life involves the possibility of

violent death, the curé enjoys an exhilarating motor-cycle ride that
represents a brief experience of physical excitement and risk in a life
committed to meditation and prayer. Olivier represents courage and
self-sacrifice through his vocation and indeed his very name: Olivier
was the companion of Roland in the Old French epic, and Tréville
the captain of Musketeers in Dumas's well-known historical novel,
so that legendary heroism and the image of the Christian soldier are
evoked through him from the outset. Delbende's name is also
significant for less literary reasons. He shares his Christian name
Maxence with one of Bernanos's closest friends from his days as a
royalist militant, Maxence de Colleville, to whom *La Grande Peur
des bien-pensants* was dedicated. To which another detail is added
by the novelist's son Jean-Loup Bernanos: namely, that his father, in
his days in the seminary of Aire-sur-la-Lys, lodged with an Abel
Delbende, the local mayor, and his three sons (*22*, p.59). Henri
Giordan records that Bernanos paid tribute to Abel Delbende's sense
of honour in a letter to a later member of the family (*9* (d), pp.119-
120). Honour is indeed Delbende's most cherished value – 'la
question sociale,' he insists, 'est d'abord une question d'honneur'
(p.1095/109) – and its rarity in the society around him has made him
too a marginal figure, in whom the curé recognises 'une blessure
profonde de l'âme' (p.1096/110). He is given an immediate human
warmth by Bernanos's portrait of a no-nonsense countryman in
corduroy trousers, living in the company of an adoring dog. He is
brusque and to the point about the curé's emaciated state and failing
health, and he too regards his patient as having a hereditary drink
problem. But the curé is pleased to be described by Delbende as
belonging to 'la même race' as Torcy and himself. A group of
kindred spirits is formed here, augmented later when Olivier
recognises in the curé 'un hors-la-loi, dans notre genre' (p.1216/258)
– for 'le bon Dieu lui-même aura du mal à distinguer des mauvais
garçons les saints de la famille' (p. 1214/255).

   What all of these soul-mates share is first of all regret at the
passing of a Christian era. It is Torcy who expresses this first, in his
homily on the great edifice of Christendom which the early Church
had set out to build: 'un empire auprès duquel celui des Césars n'eût

été que de la crotte – une paix, la Paix romaine, la vraie' (p.1044/45). He contrasts the lack of authority of 'vous autres jeunes prêtres' with the sterner leadership of their predecessors in an alleged golden age in which the Church trained its priests as 'des chefs de paroisse, des maîtres, quoi, des hommes de gouvernement' (p.1037/36). Their task, like that of the *sacristaine* in his parable, who killed herself in the vain attempt to create for her church a perfectly and permanently clean floor, can never be accomplished once and for all. The best tactic in Torcy's view is to concentrate on the simple tasks: bring straw to the ox, groom the ass. Such a practical approach to the priest's mission, eschewing the abstractions of theology, was taught, he insists, to seminarists in the good old days – a notion which leads him back in an expansive circle to his starting-point: to his vision of a militant Church and a Christian people whose common characteristics were joy and youthfulness of spirit.

Delbende, in his allusions to the Church as an army with its corporals (the ordinary members) and its field-marshals (the saints), echoes Torcy's vision of a quasi-military religious order, but whose task is unaccomplished after twenty futile centuries. This disillusionment has turned the doctor into a confirmed atheist. For him the Church is not a spiritual institution, but a bastion of social attitudes and a force for the maintenance of moral tradition. On this level, the curé naturally disagrees with Delbende. 'L'Eglise n'est pas [...] ce qu'il imagine,' he writes, 'une espèce d'Etat souverain avec ses lois, ses fonctionnaires, ses armées, – un moment, si glorieux qu'on voudra, de l'histoire des hommes' (pp.1103-04/119). Such an essentially secular view of the Church as a temporal institution identifies Delbende as a representative of the attitudes of the Action Française. Bernanos's portrait of him expresses both rejection and homage: wrong in their refusal of a religious belief, his former associates were admirable still in their defence of the values of pre-revolutionary France.

As for Olivier, he is literally a member of an army; and his regret is that the spirit which the Church is meant to represent has been allowed to wither in his institution as in others. Ambivalent as to the nature of his religious beliefs, the failure of the Church's social mission also grieves him. The Church, he says, is arguably the accomplice of injustice. It no longer opposes the corrupt attitudes of society, which he identifies as refusal, pleasure and the thirst for money; these only the soldier combats, but even the soldier's status is debased: the last true Christian soldier died on May 30th 1431 – Joan of Arc. Modern warfare, says Olivier in words that reveal in Bernanos an uncanny prophet of the destruction of Guernica, to take place within two years of the novel's composition, will become characterised by the actions of morally detached pilots, dropping their bombs on civilian populations from thirty thousand feet. And, he concludes, such mass murderers will be given the absolution of the Church more readily than the poor devil who has succumbed to sexual temptation.

Olivier's nightmare vision of mechanised warfare foreshadows Bernanos's polemical work, *La France contre le robots* (1944), and his veneration of Joan of Arc also corresponds to Bernanos's own – he had written an essay on this saint in 1934, and had even married Jeanne Talbert d'Arc, a descendant of Joan's brother (*42*, p.24). Delbende and Torcy also speak for the novelist when they express their lament for a failed Christendom and for a Church which has abdicated its responsibilities. But they represent, however movingly, the pessimistic and in some ways negative faces of Bernanos's thought, because their ideals are ossified in a past world which he knew could not be recaptured. The curé also knows this, and accordingly rises above and beyond the horizons of his companions. He disagrees with Torcy's notion of unchanging remedies for a fundamentally unchangeable society. The social policy of the Church, though its timeless mission is encapsulated in the impressive fifteenth-century church at Ambricourt, must be one of constant reassessment. Torcy by contrast, for all his charm and comic verve, appears in the first dialogue – importantly, he will change later – as a man of the previous generation. The gulf between generations is one of the central concepts in Bernanos's social thinking, identifying him not as a conservative but as a radical thinker, a man whose values are traditional but who insists on the need for each age to reformulate its strategy for relating them to the contemporary world.

Far from merely reacting to change, however, the Church in the curé's eyes is the prime agent of change. He reflects on the demise of the ancient world, based as it was on a system of slavery which the moral force of Christianity had swept away. Slavery, anti-Christian in that it threw the burden of original sin on to the backs of one social class, was the ancient world's version of injustice; but, the curé goes on, the modern world has its own form of this evil. A society 'indifférente au bien ou au mal' has been eradicated, replaced by one with 'une âme à perdre ou à sauver' (p.1066/74). But having disappeared from our laws, injustice continues to flourish in the relationships between men. Its final elimination, for the curé and for Bernanos, is the great unfinished task of the modern Church. And Bernanos's identification of where modern injustice lies introduces the second great theme of the discursive dialogues: poverty.

(iv) The eternal poor

Torcy, on reading this section of the diary, develops the curé's view of injustice to greater political depths. A different face of this complex priest appears in the second dialogue: stirred by suppressed memories, the garrulous sage is retransformed into the fervent militant he once was. No longer dreaming of a mythical Christian past, he now attacks the present-day capitalist system, which has replaced slavery while duplicating its inhumanity, and the state, which assumes in a merely half-hearted way its responsibility to the poor: 'Il torche les gosses, panse les éclopés, lave les chemises, cuit la soupe des clochards, astique le crachoir des gâteux, mais regarde la pendule et se demande si on va lui laisser le temps de s'occuper de ses propres affaires' (p.1068/76). Torcy, great metaphorist that he is, produces a memorable image here of a modern clock-watching welfare state, devoted to 'nine to five' charity.

He recalls his youth as a priest in the mining area of Norenfontes, when Pope Leo XIII's encyclical *Rerum novarum* of 1891 – famous in its day as an appeal to Catholics to involve themselves in social problems – inspired him to protest from the pulpit against the exploitation of workers, thus earning himself the reputation of a 'red' priest and banishment to another parish. His interest in the Soviet Union's social policies is thus no coincidence, although he now rejects them, for in seeking to exterminate poverty the Russians threaten the abolition of the poor: an ambition which serves the anti-Christian goals of communism, for the poor man is 'le témoin de Jésus-Christ, l'héritier du peuple juif' (p.1069/77). Torcy thus, in the great turning-point of this whole sequence, reorientates the political debate into a spiritual one, and he is followed in this by the curé, in an important parenthesis.

Here we learn of the curé's childhood experience of dire poverty, which enables him to understand the suffering of the Russian people. After his father's death, his mother had gone into hospital for the removal of a cancerous tumour, while he was entrusted to an aunt who ran a sordid bar in the mining town of Lens. The only light in this social darkness came from the books lent to him by his schoolteacher, among them the childhood memoirs of Maxim Gorky. This book, unnamed, but presumably *My Childhood*, the first volume of Gorky's autobiographical trilogy – is clearly an inspiration of his own urge to write. Like his diary, it is, in Gorky's translated words, 'the creation of a sincere artist with a passionate devotion to the truth, however cruel' (Penguin, p.25). It tells a story similar in outline to his own: that of a poor boy in Tsarist Russia, his father dead, his hapless mother unable to protect him from the brutality of other members of the family into whose charge he is placed; and it had revealed to him the existence of poverty on a vast scale: a whole nation turned, collectively, into a patron saint of *misère*. However, he had come to a very different conclusion from that of Gorky, whose angry defence of the poor had made him the literary spokesman of a Leninist regime committed, at least in theory – for Bernanos in 1936 was as blissfully unaware as most other westerners of collective farms and labour camps – to the removal of social inequalities. For the curé, what is missing from Gorky's great cry of lament is a religious dimension. His book may be a hymn to suffering, but it is not a church hymn, nor does it have any element of prayer. It inspires pity and horror, but fails to point to the one true source of alleviation, which, concludes the curé, is to be found 'sur l'épaule de Jésus-Christ' (p.1071/79).

Returning to centre-stage, Torcy relates the vulnerability of the poor man to that of the child – thus completing the thematic bridge to the first dialogue – and adds that the rich man can never be taught the virtues of childlikeness. By 'rich man', he means not just one with money and possessions, but a man possessed by the spirit of wealth. Conversely, to be poor is not just to lack material wealth; it is to embrace the spirit of poverty in a childlike trust in God's paternal love. While poverty can never be taught to the rich, the love of poverty has to be taught to the poor, for their special mission in the world is to represent to all eternity 'la pauvreté de Jésus-Christ' (p.1075/84). This is the message encapsulated in Christ's words to Judas: 'Il y aura toujours des pauvres parmi vous', which Torcy describes as 'la parole la plus triste de l'Evangile, la plus chargée de tristesse' (p.1078/88). It is nevertheless, he insists, 'la Parole, et nous l'avons reçue'.

This torrent of evangelical poetry is followed immediately by its negative counterpart in the ensuing dialogue with Blangermont, described above. Again the curé's afterthoughts provide a necessary coda to the dialogue. He realises that the *doyen*, well-known for his vigorous opposition to 'les jeunes prêtres démocrates' (p.1086/97), must put him in that category. But he is no left-wing revolutionary, no socialist priest resentful of the rich for economic reasons. He does not support class revolution, but rather a revolution of values; not the redistribution of wealth, but its relegation below the criterion of true nobility. It would be easier for him to swear allegiance to a prince or a king, deriving his authority from God through the social contract of medieval Christendom, than to a millionaire: 'La notion de richesse et celle de puissance ne peuvent encore se confondre, la première reste abstraite' (p.1086/98).

The cycle of dialogues on poverty is completed by the encounter with Delbende, who declares that 'il ne devrait plus y avoir de honte à être pauvre' (p.1095/108), and demands action from the Church to reverse the places of rich and poor within its structures. The curé, however, in a last reflective passage on the theme, argues that the kingdom of God is not of this world. Efforts to eradicate poverty are misguided, for the poor man lives, not on equality, but on the charity due to him by virtue of his poverty. Charity, he muses: 'Quel mot sublime' (p.1104/120). And he resumes the dilemma thus: 'Problème insoluble: rétablir le Pauvre dans son droit, sans l'établir dans la Puissance' (ibid.).

This formulation has force and poetic beauty as the curé's sharply honed distillation of the tortured and rambling discourse of his companions. But it may well disappoint today's readers of the novel, conscious of mass poverty on a global scale greater even than the Europe-wide concerns of Bernanos, and who still look to the Church for answers to it. Bernanos, for all his fierce onslaught on the economic corruption of our world, offers no political or economical solution to the problems he poses. He substitutes a mystical and supernatural order for that of society's institutions. As Torcy acknowledges, few poor men will find this strategy reassuring, and they might suspect Bernanos of arguing, incoherently and despite his intentions, in favour of a static paternalist state in which the leaders have the fattest pocket books. The role of the novelist, however, is perhaps best seen as to disturb rather than to offer panaceas. And in the context of this novel, the spiritual nature of the curé's conclusions on his great theme acts as a further pointer as to where the true focus of the novel lies: in a parallel world of which the events and characters described so far are merely the visible shadows. Governments, the *Journal* implies, cannot reverse the world's moral decline. What is needed, as the curé argues in his first few pages, are saints. He does not consciously realise that his own status as both poor man and spiritual child identifies him as the 'petit vacher' who can fill the saint's role in the parish and the world. Yet his destiny is a supernatural one, and every one of his relationships has to be re-read and re-examined in this light.

3. Supernatural Dramas

(i) Parallel lives

The curé's three friends are not only interlocutors in the novel's great
dialogues. Their lives are intertwined with his at a deeper, mystical
and indeed supernatural level. Torcy, for example, as well as
providing a more human face of the Church than those of the
repellingly cold doyen de Blangermont and chanoine de la Motte-
Beuvron, represents an incomplete version of the curé d'Ambricourt
himself. The events of his life foreshadow those of the curé's, albeit
on a less elevated and spiritually meaningful plane. Although
regarded by the humble curé as 'si supérieur à moi de toutes façons'
(p.1072/80), Torcy is, metaphorically speaking, a kind of John the
Baptist figure to the curé's Christ: a precursor in whose words and
experiences lie an obscure prophecy of his friend's ultimate sacrifice.
He too has known the temptation of suicide when his confidence in
himself as a priest was at a low ebb. He had survived his crisis, just
as he survives the illness which befalls him while in Lille – the place
where the curé dies from his cancer; once more, Torcy is he who has
'gone before'. He makes way for the curé to advance beyond his own
spiritual horizon in the course of their second dialogue. Seeing in him
the two qualities of poverty and childlikeness, which emerge here as
supernatural gifts qualifying their possessor for a special role in
God's providential scheme, Torcy, voice trembling and inner eye
fixed on something the curé cannot see, prophesies his colleague's
call to service in God's infantry. And as his voice falls silent, the first
stroke of the angelus is heard, 'venu de je ne sais quel point
vertigineux du ciel, comme de la cime du soir' (p.1080/91): a
portentous endorsement of the authority of a speech which, delivered
through the mouth of Torcy, seems to come from Christ himself.

Torcy, his face 'aussi noble, aussi pur, aussi paisible que celui d'un mort' (p.1080/91), is, in a sense, dead, his human personality subordinated to his role as the vehicle for 'la Parole de Dieu'. We see here, as in the later scene with the countess, Bernanos's response to one of the challenges facing the Catholic novelist: the evocation of an invisible world through the medium of flesh and blood characters.

Torcy resumes his humanity, with all its limitations, in later passages. He needs and receives the curé's healing 'regard'. 'Je l'ai regardé,' says the curé, 'comme j'ai regardé Mitonnet, ou Mademoiselle, ou...' (p.1191/227). Unable to accompany his friend on the last phase of his sacrificial mission, Torcy's role is now over: 'Nous avions l'air de nous dire adieu de loin,' writes the curé, 'd'un bord à l'autre d'une route invisible' (p.1191/227). But Torcy has one more great speech to deliver, his last in the novel. It is his evocation of the Virgin who, 'Mère par la grâce, Mère des grâces' but also 'la cadette du genre humain' in whose eyes shines 'le seul regard vraiment enfantin' (p.1194/230), is simultaneously mother and child. Torcy's final act is thus to lay the basis for the visionary experience of a few hours later, when the curé collapses by the roadside and wakes to see – or to imagine – the face of the child Mary, which is then replaced by that of Séraphita, lit by the lantern she carries as she goes, like a female equivalent of the 'petit vacher', to bring in her father's cows. Has the curé imagined the first vision? Confused the two? However we interpret it, the encounter serves again to express Bernanos's sense that the world we see is the mere surface of a spirit world beneath.

While Torcy has merely thought of suicide, Delbende goes through with it. He too enacts a potential outcome in the parallel life of the curé. His death occurs in the midst of the priest's spiritual crisis, and is sensed by him before he actually hears the news: 'Je pense à moi-même comme à un mort', he records at the end of the immediately preceding diary entry (p.1114/132). It seems to bring a strange relief; the frantic tearing of pages from his diary is succeeded by a passage marked by philosophic calm, though nevertheless curiously elliptic, leaving the impression that there are things that the diarist cannot write: that Delbende has perhaps died for him, that the suicide of the doctor whom he has met only once has had a redemptive influence on his own temptation to despair. Throughout the rest of the book and especially in the scenes with Chantal (p.1137/160) and her mother (p.1162/191), his thoughts infallibly turn to this man whose spiritual destiny merges with his own. Bernanos, once more, is suggesting through the interlinking of his characters that there is more to human life than the purely social and psychological interchange of tangible relationships; he is expressing in fictional terms his belief in the vicarious suffering of one person for others and his adherence to the doctrine of the communion of saints. Delbende, notwithstanding his atheism and his suicide – indeed, perhaps *through* his atheism and his suicide – brings succour to the curé out of all rational proportion to their brief acquaintance on this earth.

Olivier's actions also mysteriously prefigure the curé's. 'Quelle étrange coïncidence!' writes the latter on learning that Olivier has gone to Lille to spend the last days of his leave (p.1223/266) – but the reader has long since realised that in Bernanos's world nothing is coincidental. Olivier too has 'gone before', but like Torcy's his spirituality is less profound than the curé's, and his conception of death as an enemy to confront reveals a final failure of faith and trust which is perhaps remedied and compensated through the curé's own redemptive death.

(ii) The countess

The prelude to the central 'countess scene' is the curé's encounter with her daughter Chantal. Like the two Mouchette characters in other novels, Chantal is a potentially lost soul, driven towards self-destruction by the lovelessness of the world. Through her he learns of the tragic divisions in the count's family, and his diagnosis prefigures what he will say to her mother: that in responding with hatred to the faults of others, she is the accomplice of sin, a member of a communion of sinners no less real than its saintly counterpart. The scene of Chantal's confession also provides a first glimpse of the rationally inexplicable powers which have been imparted to the curé for the performance of his mission. Through the gloom of the confessional, he sees her face clearly and brightly as a foretaste of the miraculous insight he is now going to have into her intentions. As she speaks of her plan to run away, he is able to read on her lips 'd'autres mots qu'elle ne prononçait pas, qui s'inscrivaient un à un, dans mon cerveau, tout flamboyants' (p.1136/160) – miraculously revealed words that speak of her impulse to suicide. And, equally miraculously, he knows of the suicide note hidden in her closed handbag. She sees in this gift of second sight the mark of the devil; but the curé here, his stomach pain reaching new levels of intensity as he speaks, is in fact in the throes of emulating Christ.

Chantal provides the curé with one means of anticipating the problems of the countess. But another profounder means lies within himself, for he shares with her the symptoms of the inability to love. An early sign of his crisis is a feeling of lack of compassion for others, extending to a lack of pity for himself, and expressed in his anguished cry: 'Si j'allais ne plus aimer!' (p.1113/131). Before their confrontation in the château, he knows the countess's sin intimately through a mystical foreknowledge, which allows him to respond to her challenge: 'Vous avez le pouvoir de lire dans mon cœur, peut-être?' with a modest but confident 'Je crois que oui, madame' (p.1147/173). The curé is thus well placed to uncover the secret drama that lies at the origin of the family's catastrophic civil war. The couple had lost their eighteen-month old son, leaving the inconsolable countess in a pathetic world of broken toys and baby clothes, unable to love her husband and daughter, and thus driving the count into the arms of other women and their daughter to desperate flight. This is the cause, the 'faute cachée', 'le ver dans le fruit' (p.1159/188), of the evil which has contaminated this supposedly Christian household, and it typifies the strife which has demolished all the great institutions of Christendom, that 'grande famille humaine dont Notre-Seigneur est le chef' (p.1154/182). The result, the curé tells the countess, is the creation of hell on earth. The worthy middle-class may imagine hell as an abode of criminals and blasphemers, but the true hell, in Bernanos's memorable aphorism, 'c'est de ne plus aimer' (p.1157/185).

The revelation to the countess of the truth of her condition is related, not as a sweetly pious account of grace triumphant, but with the drama and suspense of an account of exorcism. The drawing of evil from her is accompanied by strange changes in her voice, which 'sans s'élever de ton, avait une sonorité bizarre, et comme un éclat métallique' (p.1160/188). As for the curé's voice, he is aware as ever of its awkwardness, of words 'prononcés si maladroitement, si gauchement qu'ils devaient paraître ridicules' (p.1157/185). What he says scarcely seems to matter. 'J'ai prononcé ces paroles,' he records, 'j'aurais pu en prononcer d'autres, cela avait à ce moment si peu d'importance' (pp.1161-62/191). It is his presence alone that affords grace the opportunity of working through him to reach the countess. In terms of Bernanos's technique, this scene is another supreme moment, capturing in fictional form the mysterious space, for a Christian or theologian, in which human agency and divine intervention converge. To the countess, it is the man, the 'rusé petit prêtre' (p.1151/178) who has moved her; he, however, feels that he is a passive means to God's end, merely 'le serviteur de tous' (p.1146/171). His humility is psychologically necessary at this moment of the novel, when, as well as leading the countess to self-evaluation, the curé too is reassured by the renewed certainty of God's presence after his long period of spiritual struggle. His description of this sense constitutes a key sentence in the novel, coming at the apex of this central episode:

> Il me semblait qu'une main mystérieuse venait d'ouvrir
> une brèche dans on ne sait quelle muraille invisible, et la
> paix rentrait de toutes parts, prenait majestueusement son
> niveau, une paix inconnue de la terre, la douce paix des
> morts, ainsi qu'une eau profonde. (p.1162/191)

The curé treads the familiar tightrope of the Bernanos priest in that his words and actions, piercing the hearts and souls of his interlocutors, provoke violent reactions on the threshold of inner peace. Donissan, in *Sous le soleil de Satan*, drives Mouchette to suicide by his dynamic revelations of her sin. The countess also responds with violence, throwing into the fire the medallion containing her dead child's lock of hair, which she now sees as a fetish to her all-consuming self-pity. The curé does not expect or demand this: 'Prenez-vous Dieu pour un bourreau?' (p. 1164/194). In thrusting his arm into the fire in an effort to retrieve the medallion, he becomes indeed an instrument in the hand of God. The drama is not over, for the countess dies in the night. Whether the curé has contributed to her death is not clear. He is suspected of so doing, and the testimony of Chantal who, having secretly observed the scene from outside the window, swears that she saw the curé force her mother to throw the medallion into the fire, pushes public opinion in its inevitable direction. But the readers of the diary, witnesses to the conflict, and aware of the joyful letter written to the curé by the countess before she dies, will be convinced by his confident statement to Torcy: 'Je l'ai laissée avec Dieu, en paix' (p.1189/224).

(iii) Laville

As his name suggests, Laville, the doctor with whom the curé has his appointment in Lille, represents the new world of the city which the country priest here encounters for the first time. The change of location in the book's third and final part is felt by the curé as a source of unease. He misses the open roads of Ambricourt, along which he had sped with Olivier a few days before, and the pure winter sky glimpsed at dawn through the window of the train which had brought him to Lille. Through Laville's window he sees only the soot-blackened walls of a narrow courtyard, and in the background he hears, not the familiar cries of cocks but the rumble of tramcars. The doctor's consulting-room also disorientates him. It is actually Laville's daughter's play-room, pressed into service while the usual office is being cleaned. The curé is surrounded, during the examination, by dislocated toys which remind us of those of the countess's dead son in the earlier scene. Here, however, the toys seem to mock his youth, and his poverty, when he strips to his much repaired undershirt, is also degraded by this new and sordid context.

Initially he is treated as brutally as the worn rag doll which Laville throws across the room in irritation; he is dismissed with no explanation of his condition, and it is only when he returns, having forgotten his prescription, and discovers Laville injecting himself with morphine, that the true confrontation with this man of the modern world begins. Laville eventually shows a kinder face, advising him how to cope with the ordeal that lies ahead – for here the curé learns for the first time that he is terminally ill, that he is not suffering from tuberculosis as he had suspected but from inoperable cancer of the stomach.

The meeting, like so many others, appears haphazard but yet is deeply significant, willed by fate or by God. It arises in the first place from a combination of confusion on the part of Delbende, who had recommended a professor Lavigne, long since retired and now deceased, and an error by the curé, who has misread the name in the telephone directory. But these apparently trivial misunderstandings have steered the curé into the presence of another suffering soul, who both resembles and crucially differs from himself. Lonely, desperate, faced like the curé by early death from a malignant disease, and tempted like him by the thought of suicide, Laville is drawn to the curé as if to his double. Struck by the physical resemblance of the curé's 'physionomie très... très remarquable' (p.1236/283) to his own, Laville speculates on all they might have in common, notably a passion for their opposed vocations, for God and Science respectively.

That Delbende should have played his part in unwittingly engineering the meeting is significant, for Laville is a kind of second version of his country co-professional, truculent and sceptical like him, but hardened by the harsher city environment. The links are deeper than this, however: when he talks of suicide, he evokes in precise detail that of Delbende – a simulated shooting accident, a rifle dragged carelessly through a hedge, a sudden bang (p.1237/285) – though in rational terms he is as ignorant of Delbende's death as of his life. Related to Delbende through the mystical network that in Bernanos's novels links the disparate members of the human family, Laville also, like Olivier, represents an alternative way of facing and imagining the experience of death in which he is fatally connected to the curé. Yet here the differences emerge. The curé has met yet another man whose destiny, like those of Olivier, Delbende and Torcy, is not as saintly as his own. He rejects Laville's suggestion of a comparison between prayer and the escape from pain and anguish which the doctor finds through drug addiction: 'On ne demande pas à la prière l'oubli,' he retorts, 'mais la force' (p.1236/284). Laville is also wrong in seeing in the curé the same resigned lack of will, the refusal to help and lead others, that he sees in himself: 'Des gens comme nous devraient rester à la queue des vaches,' he comments, marking his diametrically opposed role to that of the 'petit vacher'. So, 'prisonniers l'un de l'autre' (p.1237/286) as they may be in their mutual pain and condemnation to death, doctor and priest are not true doubles; what they have in common serves only to underline what distinguishes them: the curé's spirituality, and his belief in the theological virtue of 'espérance', so different from the notion of hope ('espoir') in medicine to which Laville's patients cling. True hope and the joy which it brings, for the sick as well as for the poor, is not to be found, Bernanos's novel proclaims, in this world but only in the next. Laville, the curé's angel of death, is taught this hard but exalting lesson by the man to whom he brings his own sombre message.

(iv) Dufréty

Dufréty is the last of the curé's false doubles, representing another alternative state, a path the curé might have followed but for God's grace. But the crucial divergences between the choices made by the two identify Dufréty as the most important of these satellite characters, his status as failed priest and self-seeking writer offering a negative image of the curé's dual vocation and underlining the latter's triumphant purity by the starkness of the contrast.

Both men have been born into poverty, and neither has climbed very far out of that state; but Dufréty rejects the spirit of poverty, and refuses to admit or embrace his social status. He pretends that his present dead-end job as a salesman for a patent drug company is merely a step on the way, a post he has temporarily chosen in preference to well-paid alternatives, and he hopes that when the curé visits him he can be received in 'un intérieur convenable, notre logement étant jusqu'ici des plus modestes' (p.1089/101). Both also suffer from poor health, but while the curé fulfils his mission despite the burden of his pain, illness for Dufréty is one more excuse for failure, a cruel affliction just when he was reaching the realisation of his ambitions. Even the nature of their respective illnesses is significant: Dufréty has tuberculosis, the disease which the curé thought he had until Laville's diagnosis of cancer; even in this, the curé is called to martyrdom above and beyond the suffering of his former friend, which is mediocre by comparison.

Mediocrity is indeed Dufréty's hallmark and the central thematic concept around which his whole character is formed. He tells the curé in his second letter that he has adopted the slogan '*Aurea mediocritas*' (p.1062/69), or golden mean, to signal his espousal of the ordinary domestic and social life into which his abandonment of the priesthood has cast him. The same phrase is used later by the curé in a context which appears quite different – that of the aim of the Soviet revolutionaries to engineer a social levelling which, in the curé's opinion, would merely produce an '*aurea mediocritas*' (p.1104/120) that would quickly provoke revolt because of its abolition of spiritual values and distinctions. Dufréty's voluntarily lack-lustre life and the faceless uniformity of the Soviet citizen might seem at first glance to have no connection, but in this novel themes are constantly interlinked in unexpected ways. The parallel ambitions of Dufréty and Communist Russia are, in spiritual terms, identical: both have abandoned the order and hierarchy willed by God. The lapsed priest and the former Mother Russia are joined in the novel by the ex-missionary Delbende and the ex-nun Mademoiselle Louise, composing a whole thematics of spiritual drop-out, to whom the failed mother and father in the château are linked by association.

Dufréty's revolt is pathetically incomplete, for he lacks the singleness of purpose to extirpate the traces of his former way of life. He greets the curé, at the door of his flat in Lille, still clad in 'un de ces pantalons de coton que nous mettons sous nos soutanes' (p.1243/292), and he carries a bottle of milk as an obscure pastiche of the holy chalice containing its transmutable wine and blood. In Dufréty's misplaced shame at his straitened economic circumstances, the curé sees the vestiges of priestly dignity, but shorn of all awareness of the spiritual meaning of the priest's status. He has fled from all that is special in the priest's role, a flight which the curé understands. The true priest pays for not being ordinary. He is a man apart, whose celibacy, representing 'la Loi' against 'les instincts' (p.1089/102), can seem inhuman and inspire both repulsion and ridicule. A good priest, writes the curé, might not incur such hostility, but the public always senses the vulnerability of the mediocre priest: 'Le prêtre médiocre est laid' (p.1089/102). The distinction is made between the bad priest and the merely mediocre one. The former would be a monster, with a particular supernatural significance, a representative of evil on the scale of Judas. Judas was special: not part of the ordinary world for which Christ refused to pray. The mediocre priest belongs to the real world as symbol and symptom of its unspectacular drift into insipid compromise and its abandonment of all the great values of Christendom. He is an accomplice of what Bernanos, throughout his entire career as a writer, presents as the modern world's particular form of evil: a shapeless and colourless entity, definable merely as the amoral absence of commitment to good. Hovering between his former state and its tepidly desired alternative, peddling cheap medicines rather than regenerative faith, sentimental rather than passionate, Dufréty exemplifies this personal and universal mediocrity in all its forms.

His very name seems to float in uncertainty. Every edition of the novel apart from the current Pocket edition, which curiously and controversially 'corrects' a famous anomaly without comment, retains what might simply seem, as Colin Nettelbeck suggests (*38*, p.181), a mere slip of the pen on the part of a novelist notorious for his textual inconsistencies: namely, the spelling 'Dupréty' the first time the curé's former friend is named (p.1057), and 'Dufréty' thereafter. The Bibliothèque Nationale manuscript throws no light on Bernanos's original choice of spelling, as the passage in which

'Duprety' is first mentioned, and indeed the whole sequence corresponding to pages 1057-80/63-91 of the novel, are missing from it. The alternative possibility, that Bernanos deliberately alters the names, is a tempting one. Names are significant in this and other novels: those of Olivier and Séraphita have been discussed above. The curé's confusion of Lavigne (symbolic of the living vine from which comes Christ's healing blood) and Laville, secular pastor of the godless town, is obviously intentional on the novelist's part. 'C'est Dieu qui nous nomme,' says Menou-Segrais to the abbé Donissan in *Sous le soleil de Satan*. 'Le nom que nous portons n'est qu'un nom d'emprunt' (p.133). 'Tous misérables,' writes Bernanos to Vallery-Radot, 'Dieu choisit parmi les médiocres des amis, [...] leur donne tout [...] jusqu'à leur nom même' (*8*, II, p.48). Ambivalent, alternative or multiple names, in his novels, often suggest disintegration or unformedness of personality, like that of souls in disarray waiting for their definitive identity to be assigned to them by God. Sabiroux/Luzarnes in *Sous le soleil de Satan* falls into this category, as does an entire gallery of characters in *Monsieur Ouine*: Philippe/Steeny, Miss/Daisy, and especially the protean comtesse de Wambescourt: Ginette/Fanny/Madame de Néréis/Jambe-de-Laine. Is it not significant that the curé himself has no name, except that of the parish, Ambricourt, to which he has given his entire essence? Does his namelessness not convey the integrity of his person and his one-ness with his flock? And might the fluctuating names of his friend be deliberate pointers to a tormented spiritual evolution, and yet another example of a seemingly trivial detail cloaking a profound supernatural mystery?

Dupréty/Dufréty is absorbed by his own evolution, that much is certain: he is writing an autobiography to plot the stages of his life. It is to be given the self-important title 'Mes Etapes', suggesting the very antithesis of the curé's opening phrase 'ma paroisse', in which the emphasis is thrown from the possessive adjective and on to the noun. Through this self-obsessed would-be writer, another series of contrasts is thus initiated, the effect of which is to reaffirm the purity of the motives of the priest/diarist. The latter reacts critically to the style even of Dufréty's letters, which he describes with thinly disguised artistic superiority as 'son pauvre discours si étudié (je crois le voir se grattant la tempe du bout de son porte-plume, comme jadis)' (p.1063/70). What Dufréty would call good writing gives to words a greater priority than truth, and again sets him apart from the curé; the mediocre priest is also a bad writer. We see nothing of his actual autobiography, but can be sure that it will be a travesty of truth, full of the same lies which characterise his letters and his conversation. He may claim to be pursuing the same end as the curé himself: sincerity. 'Je ne suis que d'un parti,' he protests: 'celui de la sincérité totale, envers les autres comme envers soi-même' (p.1247/297). Yet in the very wish to exhibit himself to others, on the grounds that they will find in his book the testimony of a 'typical' and therefore universally interesting man, Dufréty is the diametrical opposite of the curé. His 'sincerity' is judged by his own self-assured opinion, not subject like the curé's to the approval of an all-seeing divine reader and guide. Through him Bernanos seems to be alluding to the traditions of post-Christian autobiography of the type which Catholic critics like Maritain and Mauriac often associate with the name of Rousseau, and which in their eyes corrupts by its self-centred arrogance the true confessional style of the initiator of the genre, Saint Augustine. Another Bernanos character, the mayor Arsène in *Monsieur Ouine*, is described as writing his 'confessions' by candlelight, 'comme Jean-Jacques Rousseau' (p.1524). The parallel is not made specifically by the curé, to whom literary references do not come naturally; but in Dufréty one nevertheless recognises the type to which Bernanos alludes.

Dufréty's mythomaniac reconstruction of life through lies extends to his mistress, for whose natural state he clearly has no love nor respect. He pretends that she has given up a professional career for him. The woman herself, however, reveals that she is a simple working-class woman, not a doctor or even a nurse, but a former cleaning woman in the sanatorium where Dufréty had been treated, and that she now works as a daily help to keep her impoverished companion. She is nobler than him, and ready to make for him a sacrifice greater than he imagines, for she has refused his offers of marriage in case he wants to return one day to the priesthood. As he records in his diary this final dialogue of the novel, the curé hopes that the look in his eyes has communicated to her his unspoken advice: that she should leave Dufréty, let him die reconciled. For the woman herself, in her lack of a true guide who might teach her to lift her eyes towards 'le Regard de toutes les Résignations' (p.1257/310), the curé suffers. He can only hope that Torcy will help them both.

Whether the curé's dying wishes for this miserable couple are realised is another of the novel's unresolved mysteries. Dufréty's letter to Torcy reveals that the woman has now left him; we can speculate therefore that one of the curé's hopes has been fulfilled. Much less clear is whether Dufréty has been brought towards God by the encounter with his dying friend. He has certainly been pressed into service to administer the last rites to the curé, and it is he who records his friend's final moving words, borrowed by Bernanos from the writings of Saint Thérèse de Lisieux: 'Qu'est-ce que cela fait? Tout est grâce' (p.1259/313). Philippe le Touzé argues that grace is thus transmitted to Dufréty (*36*, p.268); John Flower's contrary view is that the latter 'remains uncomprehending to the end' (*13*, p.31). While the former opinion would allow the book to be read as a wholly satisfying account of the efficacy of prayer and suffering, the letter to Torcy seems on the contrary to perpetuate the image of Dufréty as a teller of half-truths at best. There is no mention in it of the diary; rather does it imply that he intends to use the diary to enhance his own would-be literary career. His style still reeks of pretence and false humility, and, most tellingly of all, it still refers to the supposed medical qualifications of his former mistress. Perhaps, in the end, Dufréty belongs to the world for which Christ will not pray; or perhaps a change in Dufréty, if ever it is destined to take place, cannot be expressed within the confines of the novel without the latter deteriorating into too rounded and too uplifting an illustration of the doctrine of reversibility of merits. Bernanos locates the access points of the supernatural; as a novelist, he has to stay on this side of the entrance.

4. Words, Things and Appearances

(i) Language

The diary embodies a commentary on the process of writing and an interrogation of language itself. It is Torcy, typically, who places language in a religious context: 'Chacun sert le bon Dieu à sa manière dans sa langue' (p.1185/220). The curé remarks at the outset on the difficult relationship between traditional religious discourse and the subtleties of modern thought: the idiom of the modern priest would be hardly recognisable by his forebears, so diluted and understated has it become. Though one can still detect 'un certain vocabulaire, d'ailleurs immuable' (p.1032/31), what has disappeared are the bold and terrifying images of persecuted saints, dripping the blood of the martyrs, indispensable rhetorical elements in sermons of yesteryear, but no longer in tune with modern taste. Middle-class Catholics, in their defence of conservative values, erode language while claiming to protect it, for they perpetuate 'un simple vocabulaire dont les termes sont si bien polis, rognés par l'usage, qu'ils justifient tout sans jamais rien remettre en question' (p.1061/68). And when such people come to confession, the same recourse to clichés conveniently dispenses them from a true examination of conscience: 'Il est si facile de ne pas se confesser du tout! [...] A force d'habitude, et avec le temps, les moins subtils finissent par se créer de toutes pièces un langage à eux, qui reste incroyablement abstrait' (pp.1099/113-14).

Expressing this, significantly, in a concrete image, the curé refers to such language as being like opaque glass, through which shines only a diffused light, conveying nothing to the eye of the shape or nature of what lies behind it. Another concrete image – the word as a door-key whose user is satisfied as long as its basic function is performed – is used to amplify an explicit, full-blown critique of language:

> C'est une des plus incompréhensibles disgrâces de l'homme, qu'il doive confier ce qu'il a de plus précieux à quelque chose d'aussi instable, d'aussi plastique, hélas, que le mot. Il faudrait beaucoup de courage pour vérifier chaque fois l'instrument, l'adapter à sa propre serrure. On aime mieux prendre le premier qui tombe sous la main, forcer un peu, et si le pêne joue, on n'en demande pas plus. (pp.1061-62/68)

Bernanos formulates here a kind of Catholic equivalent of Flaubert's onslaught on linguistic commonplaces which hide more than they reveal, though he would have argued that the implications he is drawing surpass questions of linguistic expression, since they involve a betrayal of conscience and a failure of communication with God. It is significant that this passage on the inadequacy of language directly follows the arrival of one of Dufréty's letters, and introduces the theme of good/bad writing and writers. Dufréty's language, in its self-cloaking subterfuges, is the anti-ideal against which the diarist strives. It is typical of the language which, profoundly and invidiously, acts as a barrier between men and their souls. If priests and intellectuals are responsible for creating such language, ordinary folk are no less contaminated. The curé pities the simple workmen in Mme Duplouy's café, who do not understand the dignity of their poverty in God's eyes because they lack the words in which to formulate such thoughts:

> La résignation de tous ces gens me fait honte. Elle semble d'abord n'avoir rien de surnaturel, parce qu'ils l'expriment dans leur langage, et que ce langage n'est plus chrétien. Autant dire qu'ils ne l'expriment pas, qu'ils ne s'expriment plus eux-mêmes. Ils s'en tirent avec des proverbes et des phrases de journaux. (p.1229/275)

The language of children seems to offer a respite from the doctrinally correct and uncontroversial language which the priest's role often forces him to adopt in his conversations with adults. Recalling Torcy's thought that the language of the Gospels, tender and sweet, should be reserved for communicating witĥ children (p.1073/82), he talks to them 'dans ce langage enfantin que je retrouve si vite' (p.1050/54), saying things that he has been warned not to express from the pulpit. Yet even here he is disappointed: the profoundest of all Christian words: 'amour', is sullied by the sexual awareness of the youngsters in the catechism class. The degradation of language, he remarks, is also seen in the dissemination of the slang of the trenches, 'ces affreux mots dits "de poilu"' (p.1033/31), in which he sees a trend that once more goes beyond what we would usually see as a problem of language: 'Est-ce vraiment l'argot des tranchées?' (p.1033/31). To him, it is more a symptom of a corruption of mind and spirit of which the source is deeper and less natural.

Abstraction, platitude, the rise of less welcome forms of language, represent therefore to the curé the principal threats to our means of self-expression as God's children. Faith, he argues, is not abstract and cannot be described abstractly: 'On ne saurait donner le nom de la foi à un signe abstrait, qui ne ressemble pas plus à la foi [...] que la constellation du Cygne à un cygne' (p.1126/146). Christ is no abstraction either, not some esoteric 'Dieu des spiritualistes' or a deistic 'Etre suprême', but rather the very real figure of 'ce Seigneur que nous avons appris à connaître comme un merveilleux ami vivant, qui souffre de nos peines, s'émeut de nos joies, partagera notre agonie, nous recevra dans ses bras, sur son cœur' (pp.1050-51/55).

Thus another, less obvious mission becomes apparent at the heart of the curé's diary: to refresh and refurbish language, to make it a better tool for the fashioning of an understanding of the self. Meaningless abstractions are rejected; the concrete language that we use to describe the natural world has to be harnessed to our exploration of the world of the spirit, for this is the only language comprehensible to human beings. The curé takes his first tentative steps towards fulfilling this aim in his attempt to personify abstract concepts in a sermon: his ill-fated reference to 'le regard de la paroisse' (p.1052/57), which nobody understands. He has no illusions about the difficulty of translating the fleeting states of soul through concrete words. How to describe the ebb and flow of conscience? 'Je n'ose pas dire,' he writes, 'qu'elle se décompose par-dessous, elle se pétrifie plutôt' (p.1099/114). What better word can he find for his spiritual despair than the banal 'tristesse'? 'Je ne trouve malheureusement pas d'autre mot,' he laments, 'pour qualifier une défaillance qui ne peut se définir, une véritable hémorragie de l'âme. Je m'éveillais brusquement avec, dans l'oreille, un grand cri – mais est-ce encore ce mot-là qui convient? Evidemment, non' (p.1099/114). No other word is offered. But at times a Christian language comes more easily, suggested to the curé by the inversion of our colloquial clichés. On learning that he is dying, he tells himself: 'Je savais que je garderais le silence. Garder le silence, quel mot étrange! C'est le silence qui nous garde' (p.1229/276). Finding this expression in the midst of platitude is accompanied by the curé's finding God in the midst of the café tables: 'Mon Dieu, vous l'avez voulu ainsi, j'ai reconnu votre main. J'ai cru la sentir sur mes lèvres.' The entire text of the diary records this seeking and finding of words – words to say to the countess and others, words to inscribe on paper, words to express the spiritual within the familiar context of the physical world we inhabit.

(ii) The imagery of nature

The curé's language seeks to establish the metaphysical and moral forces of good and evil as ineradicably associated components of the 'real' world of the parish, as real as physical substances like rain and mist. To achieve this, he turns to the discourse which scientists use to describe these natural phenomena. His description of the spiritual identity of his parish, for example, is couched in terminology drawn from the field of physics: 'Le bien et le mal doivent s'y faire équilibre, seulement le centre de gravité est placé bas, très bas. Ou, si vous aimez mieux, l'un et l'autre s'y superposent

[...] comme deux liquides de densité différente' (p.1031/29). Similarly, sin is described in geological imagery as a thin crust covering a subterranean cosmic reality:

> Que savons-nous du péché? Les géologues nous apprennent que le sol qui nous semble si ferme, si stable, n'est réellement qu'une mince pellicule au-dessus d'un océan de feu liquide et toujours frémissante comme la peau qui se forme sur le lait prêt à bouillir... Quelle épaisseur a le péché? A quelle profondeur faudrait-il creuser pour retrouver le gouffre d'azur? (p.1090/103)

Medical imagery also plays an important role: the parish is 'dévorée' (p.1031/29) by the moral/metaphysical phenomenon of 'ennui', which in turn is described as a form of cancer. The appropriateness of this disease as a symbol of moral decay is noted by Slava Kushnir in her perceptive study of the novel: cancer is '[la] maladie par excellence du monde moderne, considérée comme symptôme de la maladie de l'âme et qui est précisément la multiplication ou la division des cellules humaines' (*15*, p.11). For Bernanos, cancer was no mere image; it was the disease which had killed his father, and which would one day be the cause of his own death. Nor was it a merely physical enemy within the human body: announcing to Vallery-Radot the news of his father's illness, he wrote that 'ces ignobles tumeurs [...] m'ont toujours paru, plus qu'aucun autre mal, la figuration de Satan, le symbole de sa monstrueuse fécondité dans les âmes' (*8*, I, p.288). For the curé cancer is both a stark reality and also the representation of his Christ-like atonement for the sins of his parish. It is associated by him with another corrosive disease, leprosy, which is in turn identified as 'une forme turpide du désespoir' and then, in a biochemical image, as 'la fermentation d'un christianisme décomposé' (p.1032/31).

The evil that lurks within disease is also found in other dimensions of physical nature. Even a climatic feature such as 'le ciel hideux de novembre' (p.1031/29) carries a direct supernatural significance: the lowering sky contains not just dark clouds, but the essence of evil. Black water and mud are similar indicators of evil's presence: sin is described as 'une eau noire et profonde' and, in an image drawn from the Book of Revelations (20. 14-15), sinners coagulate together to form 'ce lac de boue toujours gluant sur quoi passe et repasse vainement l'immense marée de l'amour divin, la mer de flammes vivantes et rugissantes qui a fécondé le chaos' (p.1139/163). Darkness and night (the time, according to Torcy, when the devil undoes all the order created during the day) have similar semantic functions: 'Je respire, j'aspire la nuit,' writes the curé in the midst of his despair, 'la nuit entre en moi par je ne sais quelle inconcevable, quelle inimaginable brèche de l'âme. Je suis moi-même nuit' (p.1113/130). By extension, his life is like a 'mur noir' (p.1111/128), until it is penetrated, in the scene with the countess, by God's grace, entering through another 'brèche' (p.1162/191) or access point of the supernatural.

Behind this rolling cycle of descriptive and metaphorical discourse lies the deep meaning of Bernanos's writing. Between 'reality' in his augmented sense of that term and language there is not the usual gap between signified and signifier of which linguists and literary critics speak; words and images are not so much symbols as symptoms of the state of fallen nature. The natural phenomena that language describes are likewise not just shadowy metaphors for the spirit world. The rain and mist of northern France, 'qu'on avale à pleins poumons, qui vous descendent jusqu'au ventre' and which are transformed into 'une espèce de poussière [que] vous [...] respirez, [...] mangez [...], buvez' (pp.1032/29-30), do not just 'represent' the 'cancer' of the 'ennui' that is 'en nous'; they *are* that 'ennui', and what we swallow is that 'ennui' itself – just as for the Catholic Bernanos, what is swallowed in the Mass are not symbols of Christ's body and blood, but their substance.

This parallel leads us to the recurring references to the curé's enforced diet of bread and wine, which illustrate perfectly the impossibility of distinguishing in Bernanos between metaphor and the literal transcription of 'higher' reality. On one level, one could say that these references remind us of the Mass, and that they suggest that the curé's life, metaphorically speaking, is a perpetual communion with Christ. Yet to label these terms as metaphors is to undervalue their role in the text. For what is really suggested is that the curé's wine is a true spiritual beverage, that he is literally slaking his thirst on the blood of Christ. Unlike normal wines, which, in the colloquial saying, 'ne supportent pas le voyage' (p.1034/32), his 'seems to be embarked on its own itinerary, transforming itself from its original state into a new one. He himself notices its strangeness: 'Il m'a paru un peu trouble, néanmoins il embaume' (p.1053/57). When the count chances to taste it, he too finds it peculiar, but merely comments that it is 'aigre', that drinking it is 'malsain' (p.1124/144). The more forthright Torcy comes closest to speaking the truth, calling the wine 'une affreuse teinture', but without appreciating the literal sense of his own words: 'Ce n'est pas du vin' (p.1190/225). The author's prompting could hardly be more direct. What he implies is that, just as there is no coincidence, so is there no metaphor; all is real, and 'tout est grâce'. His understanding of the representational powers of language is ultimately inseparable from his theology.

The motor-cycle ride with Olivier can also be interpreted in the same literal terms as an alternative journey into a domain of purity and light, foreshadowing, not just metaphorically, the curé's death and access to paradise. The ride takes place on a 'triomphal matin' (p.1211/251); it opens 'la porte d'un autre monde' (p.1213/253); it is '[une] prodigieuse ascension' (ibid.). As the bike cuts through 'un paysage [qui] s'ouvrait de toutes parts' (ibid.), the previous image of the two horizontal layers of good and evil which constitute our moral universe is echoed in spatially altered form, reorientated on to a vertical axis:

> J'étais bien incapable de mesurer le chemin parcouru, ni
> le temps. Je sais seulement que nous allions vite, très
> vite, de plus en plus vite. Le vent de la course n'était
> plus, comme au début, l'obstacle auquel je m'appuyais
> de tout mon poids, il était devenu un couloir vertigineux,
> un vide entre deux colonnes d'air brassées à une vitesse
> foudroyante. Je les sentais rouler à ma droite et à ma

gauche, pareilles à deux murailles liquides, et lorsque j'essayais d'écarter le bras, il était plaqué à mon flanc par une force irrésistible. (pp.1213/253-54)

The curé's exhilaration not only produces visual distortion – 'L'immense horizon a vacillé...' (p.1213/254) – but also release from the depressing horizontality of the moral layers of earthly existence. Vertical columns of air rise on both sides, and the centripetal force of the ride pins his arm and body into a vertical position. When it is over, 'le ciel s'était couvert' (p.1213/254); he has returned from a world where everything points heavenwards, back to the earth where all is flat and featureless, and on which he is destined to live for only a few more days. 'J'ai bien senti,' he writes, 'que je m'éveillais d'un rêve' (p.1213/254). This return to reality illustrates again the proximity of the two worlds, the presence of a spiritual dimension just above or below the plane of our visible lives.

(iii) 'Object lessons'

The world of nature is full not just of people but of things. The curé is constantly aware of objects around him, inseparable parts of his total experience of living, and witnesses to his inner feelings: 'Je regarde avec stupeur ma fenêtre ouverte sur la nuit, le désordre de ma table, les mille petits signes visibles à mes yeux seuls où s'inscrit comme en un mystérieux langage la grande angoisse de ces dernières heures' (p.1183/217). Even his diary exists as a physical object, its familiar presence a comfort in its own right even when he cannot find words to write in it. In periods of spiritual difficulty, 'ces feuilles de papier blanc' (p.1131/153) and even the table on which they lie are a comfort to him in their solidity and certainty.

Novelists since before Balzac's time have famously used physical objects for both descriptive and symbolical purposes. Things are central to our awareness of life; they are part of the texture of reality. Realist or Naturalist novelists like the Goncourts and Zola were so intent on capturing that texture that objects, in their novels, so proliferate as to crowd out the invisible and intangible world in which Christians believe. The challenge to Christian beliefs and values constituted by the Realist novel is thus embodied in its descriptive techniques. Bernanos's aspiration to a 'Christian realism' involves coming to terms with this historical challenge, and assigning to objects, these prime indicators of the real, a role in the production of a Christian meaning within his novels (see *41, passim*).

As so often, it is an aphorism of Torcy's which introduces this theme. He expresses his joy in offering to children a spiritual education so unlike the one they receive in their lay school: 'des problèmes de fractions, du droit civique, ou encore de ces abominables leçons de choses, qui ne sont en effet que des leçons de choses et rien de plus. L'homme à l'école des choses!' (p.1050/54). As well as his scorn of such 'object lessons', which teach only of the surface of life, his indifference to the appearance of objects is also made clear by the description of the low aesthetic quality of the religious ornaments and artefacts which decorate Torcy's room: 'un assez vilain chromo [...] qui représente un Enfant Jésus bien joufflu, bien rose, entre l'âne et le bœuf' (p.1041/42). Flaubert and Zola had made great polemical capital from the contrast between sublime faith and such unimpressive visual images; but in Torcy, such simplicity and aloofness to material values ennoble rather than demean. The objects which surround him are less important than those he conjures up in his speech, as images of means to God's ends. He compares the word of God to a red-hot iron, a 'fer rouge' which burns first and consoles afterwards. 'Toi qui l'enseignes [la parole],' he challenges the curé, 'tu voudrais la prendre avec des pincettes, de peur de te brûler, tu ne l'empoignerais pas à pleines mains?' (p.1071/80). These are prophetic words whose meaning is revealed in the scene with the countess – a scene which offers a sustained illustration of the role of objects in Bernanos's fiction.

From its opening lines, familiar scenes and objects are used to hold in balance the supernatural and realist levels of the narrative. They are justified, on the surface, by the curé's conscious grasping of them as props in his agitation; and they punctuate the whole scene, from his perception of the gardener piling up dead wood, to the familiarity of the breakfast table and other furniture, and the homely spluttering of a log fire:

> Mon agitation était si grande qu'à l'entrée du parc, je me suis arrêté longtemps pour regarder le vieux jardinier Clovis fagotant du bois mort comme à l'ordinaire. Son calme me faisait du bien.
> [..]
> Par la porte entrebâillée, je voyais la table dressée pour la collation matinale, et qu'on venait de quitter sans doute. J'ai voulu compter les tasses, les chiffres se brouillaient dans ma tête.
> [...]
> Elle m'a désigné un siège, je ne le voyais pas, elle a fini par le pousser elle-même jusqu'à moi. (p.1145/170)

> Les bûches sifflaient dans l'âtre. Par la fenêtre ouverte, à travers les rideaux de linon, on voyait l'immense pelouse fermée par la muraille noire des pins, sous un ciel taciturne. (p.1146/172)

At moments like this, where the supernatural drama is at its highest, the counter-movement of realist detail, anchoring the scene in a familiar atmosphere, is most necessary. As he confronts the countess in the great struggle for her soul, the curé is aware of the sounds of glasses being washed in the kitchen, of rain beating on a window pane: 'Tout était calme, facile, familier' (p.1149/176). Above all, he is conscious of the poker in the hands of the countess, as she distractedly plays with the burning logs in the fireplace. Here is the 'fer rouge' of which Torcy had spoken, the 'thing' of which the curé himself is another example. He tells the countess:

> On est toujours le serviteur de quelqu'un. Moi, je suis le serviteur de tous. Et encore, serviteur est-il un mot trop noble pour un malheureux petit prêtre tel que moi, je devrais dire la chose de tous, ou moins même, s'il plaît à Dieu. – Peut-on être moins qu'une chose? (p.1146/171)

He literally becomes a thing, a poker, a 'fer rouge' – and by extension, the embodiment of God's word which Torcy had identified the latter as being – when, rising to Torcy's forgotten challenge, he plunges his arm into the fire to retrieve the medallion. The substitution of man for thing is made quite explicit in the curé's words to the countess:

> Ce tisonnier n'est qu'un instrument dans vos mains. Si le bon Dieu lui avait donné juste assez de connaissance pour se mettre de lui-même à votre portée, lorsque vous en avez besoin, ce serait à peu près ce que je suis pour vous tous, ce que je voudrais être. (p.1146/171)

In this utter sacrifice of himself to God's will, this willing transformation of his person into the tool of God's purpose, the curé reaches the point at which flesh and spirit are indistinguishable, and where the physical world is permeated by grace.

(iv) Bodies and souls

We have seen that in Bernanos's new 'Catholic realism' the physical world, far from vanquishing the world of the spirit by simply outweighing it – as it does in traditional nineteenth-century Realism – is the means of access to it. This is true not just of objects, but also of his physical portrayal of human beings. He seems remarkably uninterested in describing the appearance of his characters for its own sake, and much more concerned to focus on those aspects which reveal or suggest what is happening beneath the flesh and blood surface. The reader of the *Journal* is given little help in visualising the characters. At best a few impressions may remain when we close the book: of the curé himself as a dark and emaciated young man, 'un noiraud du Boulonnais' as Torcy describes him (p.1042/42) – an impression only once extended into a full facial portrait when the curé glimpses himself in the mirror in Delbende's house and is struck by '[son] triste visage, un peu plus jaune chaque jour, avec ce long nez, la double ride profonde qui descend jusqu'aux commissures des lèvres, la barbe rase mais dure...' (p.1092/105). 'Triste' is a frequent adjective for the curé's face and, like the entire portrait, tells us more of his inner being than his visual appearance. The same is true of descriptions of various characters. Torcy is said to have 'un air d'assurance et de commandement' (p.1043/44); his face expresses 'beaucoup de tendresse et [...] une espèce d'inquiétude, d'anxiété' (p.1040/40). Of Sulpice's face, all we know is that it reveals 'la volonté du mensonge' that is in his heart (p.1124/145). As E.-A. Hubert comments, there is little continuation in Bernanos's novels of the Balzacian tradition of global portraiture:

> Les personnages n'y font jamais l'objet d'une description suivie et, seules, quelques notations interviennent, suscitées par le mouvement profond du roman. Très rares sont d'ailleurs dans l'œuvre de Bernanos les notations statiques, c'est-à-dire celles qui concernent l'aspect permanent du personnage, indépendamment du drame qui se joue. (*9* (b), p. 29)

Even the colours of characters' eyes seem chosen to reflect mood or inner state: the countess's are grey, and so are Séraphita's; the blue eyes of both Olivier and Dufréty's mistress suggest the survival of the child within them – although in Olivier's case his eyes are hard to describe: 'si pâles qu'on n'en saurait dire la couleur exacte' (p.1210/251). The fundamental mystery of human character seems encapsulated in the apparent unwillingness of eyes and faces to be fixed, photographically, once and for all. They are more often caught in a fleeting moment of transition:

> Le visage de M. le comte a changé si vite que je n'en croyais pas mes yeux. Il semblait horriblement gêné. Elle [Chantal] le regardait d'un air triste... (p.1179/212)

> Le visage de cette petite [Séraphita] me semble se transformer de jour en jour: jadis si changeant, si mobile... (p.1053/58)

> Sa maigre petite figure [Séraphita again] n'était guère
> moins rusée que d'habitude, mais ce que j'y remarquai
> d'abord était un air de gravité douce, un peu solennelle,
> presque comique... (p.1199/237)

Hands are also important as indicators of struggles within. The
countess's 'faisaient le geste de se raccrocher, de se soutenir à
quelque chose d'invisible' (p.1150/176); 'sa main s'était crispée
autour d'un vieil éventail...' (p.1151/178) – the same broken fan that
the curé finds on the morning after her death, an objective symbol of
the anguish of their encounter. Her dead hands 'croisées, [...] très
fines, très longues, plus vraiment mortes que le visage' (p.1169/200),
express her beauty in final repose. They relate to the fingers of the
curé's mother, chaffed from countless washing days, unable to turn
the pages in her old copy of the *Imitation* (p.1166/196). Touching
too is Torcy's worn old hand, 'enflée par la diabète' (p.1040/40).
The hands of the Virgin, in the vision scene, are conventionally
'pleines de grâces', but they are also the hands of a poor child
(p.1197/234).

In these and other examples of physical portraiture Bernanos
has turned the novelist's notations of appearances into means of
suggesting a dimension beneath the surface. The reader is simply
given outer clues to inner events. He is in the same situation as the
abbé Menou-Segrais in *Sous le soleil de Satan* who 'ne démêlait qu'à
demi' the hidden conflicts in his young protégé Donissan, for he was
privy only to the 'signes physiques' which show on the uppermost
layer of being (p.135). Of the crucial, inner drama, 'rien ne paraîtra
plus au-dehors, jamais' (p.137). Bernanos's *bête noire*, Emile Zola,
had inaugurated a language of the body, a notion of a 'physiological'
man more open to the exploration of the scientist than the allegedly
outmoded Christian model of man, imbued with an immortal soul. In
Bernanos, the body is the soul's envelope, and his description of it
gives it that limited status. Thus his use of language runs parallel to
his religious conviction, and in the end is inseparable from it.

Conclusion

The threads of this powerful novel are brought together in the final pages relating the curé's death in Dufréty's flat. His humility is such that he continues to regard himself as inferior to his erstwhile companions because their attitude to death would be one of great courage. His own attitude, he says, is neither to fear nor to embrace death, but to humbly contemplate its 'regard'. Repeating the self-same words that he had applied to Torcy on their last encounter, the curé writes that he looks at death 'comme j'avais regardé Sulpice Mitonnet, ou Madame Chantal' (p.1256/308). Death itself, because it too is part of God's scheme, is embraced with a kind of charity, its sting removed by the curé's utter acceptance. The reader knows that this humility is the sign of the curé's special election, and that his total lack of pride prevents him applying to himself his moving words on the simple and poor: 'Mais les gens du monde disent "les simples" comme ils disent "les humbles", avec le meme sourire indulgent. Ils devraient dire: les rois!' (p.1245/295).

The final death scene underlines his status as Christian 'king' in this sense and distinguishes him from his partial *alter egos*. The ugliness of Dufréty's flat, this Golgotha to which has led his journey from the Nazareth of Ambricourt to the Jerusalem that is Lille, provokes a short-lived revolt against his physical fate – 'Je ne veux pas mourir ici!' (p.1246/296) – which is also a part of the imitation of Christ which he is called to fulfil. He regains control, accepting that he was meant by God to die young. Like Christ, he can forgive the unjust: '*Non sciunt quod facient*' (p.1255/307). The child-curé here absolves the world of its injustice to the curé-poor man, and at the same time achieves final reconciliation with himself, self-hate gone, self-love purified. Simple faith, hope and love – pure love of self as well as love for others – are the values expressed in the closing words of the diary:

Il est plus facile que l'on croit de se haïr. La grâce est de
s'oublier. Mais si tout orgueil était mort en nous, la grâce
des grâces serait de s'aimer humblement soi-même,
comme n'importe lequel des membres souffrants de
Jésus-Christ. (p.1258/311)

The inadequacy of the plot summary of *Journal d'un curé de
campagne* that was sketched at the beginning of this guide is now
clear. It was couched in social and psychological terms, and based on
the surface events of his life as described by the curé. But the curé
warns us: 'Comme nous savons peu ce qu'est réellement une vie
humaine! La nôtre. Nous juger sur ce que nous appelons nos actes est
peut-être aussi vain que de nous juger sur nos rêves' (1100/114).
There is a deeper plot, transcending action and translating
Bernanos's conviction that the spiritual destinies of human beings are
worked out on an invisible plane which the rational mind cannot
grasp. This alternative plot would trace the vicarious links which
bind the curé to the other characters: the mutual inspiration between
him and Torcy, the death of Delbende which, as a substitution for the
suicidal act which the curé is contemplating, mysteriously stays that
self-destructive urge; the courage of Olivier which helps him to face
death; his guiding of the countess to reconciliation with God; his
encounter with his false doubles Laville and Dufréty; his suffering as
an innocent child or 'petit vacher' on behalf of all the poor of the
world with whom the archetype of the child is mystically linked; and
his final simple acceptance of death as an element in the providential
grace of God which penetrates all people and all things. Bernanos
refrains from overclarification of these relationships, for in that
direction lies the danger of arrogant preaching, or even the
presumption of knowing the mind of God. The origin, meaning and
outcome of the multiple and interlocking spiritual dramas in which
the curé is mystically linked with Delbende, the countess and Dufréty
are ultimately unknowable, and can only be suggested through the
subtle promptings of the text. What emerges clearly, however, is the
conviction, central to all of Bernanos's writing, that the key to human

experience, personal and collective, moral and political, is to be found not in a social dimension but in a supernatural one.

Does this mean, in the end, that one has to be a Christian or even a Catholic to enter into this novel? Clearly not. One merely has to read the testimony of André Malraux, far removed from Bernanos in his view of the nature of reality, who yet refers to the latter, in his preface to the Pocket edition of the *Journal*, as 'le plus grand romancier de son temps' (p.15). Attempts have been made to reinterpret Bernanos afresh, and from outside his own Christian grid of reference. Perhaps the most successful of these in recent times is Slava Kushnir's essay, *Le Héros et son double*, which relates the *Journal* to other types of 'myth', and presents the curé as a man embarked on an initiatic journey of self-discovery, in which he has to free himself from the influence of old mentors and confront the 'mauvaise Mère' – the countess – before coming fully to terms with his own separate identity. The problem, even with such a brilliant re-reading of the text, is that while it might function as an analysis of plot, it does not cope with the religious depths of theme or character.

What makes the novel accessible, ultimately, is the first-person narrative form in which it is couched. In 'Catholic' novels written in traditional third-person form, the responsibility for conveying the novelist's religious perceptions is devolved to the narrator; thus, presumptions of God's role in the affairs of human beings are written into the fabric of the entire text, and for readers unable to accept them, the novel as a whole risks rejection. In *Journal d'un curé de campagne*, the experience of religious emotion – doubt, despair, joy – is conveyed wholly from within the central character, as a psychological strand within the fiction. The reader might deny the basis of the beliefs on which that experience rests, and find alien the notion that 'tout est grâce', yet still be wholly persuaded by the emotive power of the curé's portrait and the reality of the world he inhabits. It is the encounter with the suffering young priest and his attempts to make sense of his fate that constitutes for most readers the accessibility and indeed universality of Bernanos's text.

APPENDIX

From Word to Image: Bresson's Film

Before his death Bernanos refused to sanction two previous proposals for film versions of *Journal d'un curé de campagne*, the first from the Dominican R.-L. Bruckberger (who was later responsible for a poorly received film of *Dialogues des Carmélites*), the second from J. Aurenche. The latter's script in particular, opening with scenes of Chantal spitting out a communion wafer, which the curé picks up and swallows, and ending on a version of the encounter with Arsène in which the old man utters the final words: 'Quand on est mort, tout est mort', so offended Bernanos that he denounced it as a travesty and betrayal of the novel in a letter to the newspaper *Samedi soir* (*46*, p.20).

Robert Bresson's film, had Bernanos lived to see it, would certainly have met with a different response from the novelist. The author of previous screen adaptations of novels and of films on religious subjects, Bresson treats the *Journal* with a profound concern to keep faith with his source material. The very text of the novel, as can be seen by comparing with it the extracts from the scenario published in Michel Estève's book on Bresson, is used as the basis both for the film's dialogues and for the 'voice-off' commentary that accompanies the shots of the curé writing his diary. The setting is projected with a grainy realism, and the intense emotional dramas of the curé and the count's family are conveyed with a conviction that arises partly from the producer's use of unknown actors for the principal roles – only Marie-Monique Arkel (the countess) and Antoine Balprêtré (Delbende) were familiar faces to the cinema public of 1950.

The reader of the *Journal*, therefore, might turn to this film, still occasionally shown on television in France and elsewhere, as a visual reinforcement of the reading of the novel's dense text. It must be remembered, however, that this is not the 'film of the book', but an independent work of art that takes Bernanos as its source. Bresson's art, as Estève points out (*46*, p.22), is more sober than that of Bernanos. The rich metaphorical language of the novel, while often heard in the film's commentary, is not transposed into equivalent images. Bresson's film reduces the layers of the text to its basic essentials, with everything omitted that does not directly relate to the presentation of the central character. The social and historical dimensions of the novel are sacrificed, and with them much of what Estève calls Bernanos's 'prophétisme' (*46*, p.33). Paradoxically the omissions can be said to serve the reader best by drawing attention to what is most unique and irreplaceable in the novel itself. In addition, the narrative structure undergoes some distortion. The central scene is no longer the countess scene, which is rather underplayed, but the encounter between the curé and Torcy in Clovis's hut, where the curé's vocation, understandably difficult for Bresson to express in cinematic terms, is simply revealed to him by the words of his older colleague: 'Et tout à coup Notre Seigneur me faisait la grâce de m'apprendre par la bouche de mon vieux maître que rien ne m'arracherait à la place choisie pour moi de toute éternité, que j'étais prisonnier de la Sainte Agonie' (*46*, p.26).

Such divergences apart, Bresson's direction is painstakingly faithful to the spirit of the original, and the camera-work of Léonce-Henri Burel and the performance of Claude Laydu as the curé combine to produce a memorable tribute to the power and inspiration of the *Journal*. The contrast of light and dark – the image of a crucifix invariably shot in shadow to suggest the difficulty of access to God's will, the radiance of Laydu's emaciated features – is forever striking. The atmosphere of the village is well conveyed, as is that of the city of Lille: an invention of producer and cameraman together is the fine shot in which the curé, crossing a road, is caught between two monstrous tramcars, visual symbols of the dehumanised industrial world. Even here, however, as Estève, always an authoritative commentator on the relationship of book to film, remarks, Bresson 'ne relie pas cette perte du sens de l'humain à un phénomène de déchristianisation' (*46*, p.33). For that, and for all that is central to Bernanos's genius, the reader must return, definitively, to the novel.

Select Bibliography

Sections A-C are arranged chronologically, the other sections alphabetically by author. Unless otherwise stated, all French books were published in Paris, and all books in English, and editions with English introduction and notes, in London. *Journal d'un curé de campagne* has been abbreviated to *JCC* throughout.

A. SOME EDITIONS OF JCC

1. *JCC*, Plon, 1936. The original edition.
2. *JCC*, Le Livre de Poche, 1963 (with numerous reprints).
3. *JCC*, edited by E.M. O'Sharkey, University of London Press, 1969.
4. *JCC*, in *Œuvres romanesques; Dialogues des Carmélites*, préface par Gaëtan Picon, texte et variantes établis par Albert Béguin, notes par Michel Estève, Bibliothèque de la Pléiade, Gallimard, 1980, pp.1029-1259.
5. *JCC*, préface inédite d'André Malraux, notice bibliographique de Jean-Loup Bernanos, Pocket, 1984.

B. BOOKS BY BERNANOS, OTHER THAN NOVELS, REFERRED TO IN THIS GUIDE

6. *La Grande Peur des bien-pensants*, in *Essais et écrits de combat*, textes présentés et annotés par Yves Bridel, Jacques Chabot et Joseph Jurt sous la direction de Michel Estève, Bibliothèque de la Pléiade, Gallimard, 1971.
7. *Les Grands Cimetières sous la lune*, in *Essais et écrits de combat*, ed. cit.
8. *Correspondance inédite*, recueillie par Albert Béguin, choisie et présentée par Jean Murray, O.P., Plon, 1971: 2 volumes: I. *Combat pour la vérité*; II. *Combat pour la liberté*.

C. COLLECTIONS OF ARTICLES

9. *Etudes bernanosiennes*, Minard, La Revue des Lettres Modernes, vol. 2, 1961-62, a number wholly dedicated to *JCC*, and containing the following articles:
   (a) M. Estève, 'Genèse du *JCC*', pp.3-16
   (b) E.-A. Hubert, 'L'Expression romanesque du surnaturel dans le *JCC*', pp.17-54
   (c) N. Winter, 'Conception bernanosienne du sacerdoce à partir du *JCC*', pp.55-84
   (d) H. Giordan, 'La Réalité sociale et politique dans le *JCC*', pp.85-121
   (e) A. Béguin, 'Appendice: notes sur le "bestiaire" du *JCC*', pp.122-25
10. *Etudes bernanosiennes*, vol. 18, 1986, primarily on *JCC*, containing:
    (a) P. Copiz, 'Le Brouillon manuscrit de *JCC*', pp.7-16
    (b) T. Yucel, 'Dialogues du curé d'Ambricourt – le temps, l'espace et l'être', pp.17-32
    (c) R. Rechou, 'Note sur le procédé du journal intime', pp.33-42
    (d) P. Gille, 'Roman et histoire d'après *JCC* – note sur la diachronie du texte romanesque', pp.43-56
    (e) C. Garda, 'La nuit dans *JCC*', pp.57-86
    (f) M. Estève, 'La Nuit de Gethsémani', pp.87-108
    (g) A. Pennicaud, 'Approches de la vision bernanosienne de la pauvreté', pp.109-32

N.B. The whole series of the *Etudes bernanosiennes* (20 volumes to date) is well worth consulting, as many numbers contain individual articles on or relevant to *JCC*. Another regular series is *Les Cahiers Georges Bernanos*, published annually since 1991 by the Association Internationale des Amis de Georges Bernanos.

D. BOOKS ON JCC

11. H. Aaraas, *A propos du JCC: essai sur l'écrivain et le prêtre dans l'œuvre romanesque de Bernanos*, Minard, 1966.
12. D.W. Chao, *Le Style du JCC*, Washington DC: University Press of America, 1981.
13. J.E. Flower, *Bernanos: JCC*, Edward Arnold, Studies in French Literature, 16, 1970.
14. G. Hoffbeck, *JCC de Bernanos*, Hachette, Poche Critique, 1972.
15. S.M. Kushnir, *Le Héros et son double: essai sur le JCC de Georges Bernanos*, Sherbrooke (Canada): Naaman, 1984.
16. R. Mathé, *JCC, Bernanos*, Hatier, 1970.

17. D. Renaud. *JCC, Georges Bernanos*. Nathan. collection 'Balises'. 1993.

E. BOOKS WITH IMPORTANT SECTIONS ON JCC

The following is a strictly selective list from the large body of critical literature on Bernanos:

18. H. Aaraas. *Sacerdoce et littérature*. Minard. 1984.
19. S. Albouy. *Bernanos et la politique*. Privat. 1980.
20. H. U. von Balthasar. *Le Chrétien Bernanos*. Seuil. 1954.
21. A. Béguin. *Bernanos par lui-même*. Seuil. 1982.
22. J.-L. Bernanos. *Georges Bernanos à la merci des passants*. Plon. 1986.
23. G. Blumenthal. *The Poetic Imagination of Georges Bernanos*. Baltimore: Johns Hopkins Press. 1965.
24. Y. Bridel. *L'Esprit d'enfance dans l'œuvre romanesque de Georges Bernanos*. Minard. 1966.
25. W. Bush. *Souffrance et expiation dans la pensée de Bernanos*. Minard. 1962.
26. J. Chéry-Aynesworth. *Approche rhétorique de la dialectique des sens chez Bernanos*. 2 vols. Minard. 1982-83.
27. A.R. Clark. *La France dans l'histoire selon Bernanos*. Minard. 1983.
28. H. Debluë. *Les Romans de Georges Bernanos ou le défi du rêve*. Neuchâtel: La Baconnière. 1965.
29. M. Estève. *Bernanos: un triple itinéraire*. Hachette. 1981.
30. B.T. Fitch. *Dimensions et structures chez Bernanos, essai de méthode critique*. Minard. 1969.
31. G. Gaucher. *Le Thème de la mort dans les romans de Georges Bernanos*. Minard. 1967.
32. P. Gille. *Bernanos et l'angoisse*. Nancy: Presses Universitaires. 1984.
33. M. Gosselin. *L'Ecriture du surnaturel dans l'œuvre romanesque de Georges Bernanos*. Champion. 1979.
34. E. Lagadec-Sadoulet. *Temps et récit dans l'œuvre de Georges Bernanos*. Klincksieck. 1988.
35. G. Leclerc. *Avec Bernanos*. Albin Michel. 1982.
36. P. Le Touzé. *Le Mystère du réel dans les romans de Georges Bernanos*. Nizet. 1979.
37. M. Milner. *Georges Bernanos*. Desclée de Brouwer. 1967.
38. C. Nettelbeck. *Les Personnages de Bernanos romancier*. Minard. 1970.
39. G. Poulet. *Le Point de départ*. Plon. 1964.
40. J. Scheidegger. *Georges Bernanos romancier*. Neuchâtel: Attinger. 1956.

41. M. Scott. *The Struggle for the Soul of the French Novel: French Catholic and Realist novelists 1850-1970.* Macmillan. 1989. especially chapter 8. 'The Bernanosian Synthesis'. pp.237-66.

42. R. Speaight. *Georges Bernanos, a Study of the Man and the Writer.* Collins & Harvill. 1973.

43. J.C. Whitehouse. *Le Réalisme dans les romans de Georges Bernanos.* Minard. 1969.

F. STUDIES OF BRESSON'S FILM

44. A. Bazin. 'Le *JCC* et la stylistique de Robert Bresson'. *Cahiers du Cinéma.* no. 3. June 1951. in *Qu'est-ce que le cinéma?.* Editions du Cerf. 1959.

45. A. Béguin. 'Bernanos au cinéma'. *Esprit.* February 1951.

46. M. Estève. *Robert Bresson.* Cinéma d'Aujourd'hui. no. 8. Editions Seghers. 1962. Contains substantial extracts of the screenplay.

CRITICAL GUIDES TO FRENCH TEXTS

edited by

Roger Little, Wolfgang van Emden, David Williams